The Unimaginable Loss

THE UNIMAGINABLE LOSS

A MOTHER'S THOUGHTS ON THE LOSS OF A CHILD

Fiona McWilliams

The Book Guild Ltd

First published in Great Britain in 2019 by
The Book Guild Ltd
9 Priory Business Park
Wistow Road, Kibworth
Leicestershire, LE8 0RX
Freephone: 0800 999 2982
www.bookguild.co.uk
Email: info@bookguild.co.uk
Twitter: @bookguild

Copyright © 2019 Fiona McWilliams

The right of Fiona McWilliams to be identified as the author of this
work has been asserted by her in accordance with the
Copyright, Design and Patents Act 1988.

All rights reserved. No part of this publication may be
reproduced, transmitted, or stored in a retrieval system, in any form or by any means,
without permission in writing from the publisher, nor be otherwise circulated in
any form of binding or cover other than that in which it is published and without
a similar condition being imposed on the subsequent purchaser.

Typeset in Adobe Garamond Pro

Printed and bound in the UK by TJ International, Padstow, Cornwall

ISBN 978 1912881 697

British Library Cataloguing in Publication Data.
A catalogue record for this book is available from the British Library.

For Belle
Isabelle Docherty
1998–2016

———

For Mark and Cara
We walk the same line

CONTENTS

1. Incomprehensible Tragedy — 1
2. Early Days After The Funeral — 10
3. Practicalities – Dealing With Things And Sorting Things Out — 26
4. Grief Is Not A Journey — 34
5. Counselling — 52
6. Living With Grief — 58
7. Memorial and Commemoration Services — 72
8. Dealing With Death – The Myth Of Closure — 75
9. Your Relationship — 79
10. Your Other Children – Sibling Survival — 85

11. Grief, Long-Term	90
12. Finding The Future	97
13. No Rules	102
Thank You	105
Sources of Help	108
Endnotes	111

1

INCOMPREHENSIBLE TRAGEDY

"Grief" is defined as "intense sorrow, especially caused by someone's death" and suggested synonyms include "sorrow, misery, sadness, anguish, pain, distress, agony, torment, affliction, suffering, heartache, heartbreak, broken-heartedness, heaviness of heart, woe, desolation, despondency, dejection, despair, angst".

When my daughter died, I felt all of these – there can be no one word to describe the awfulness of losing a child.

How do we survive such loss? Everyone's experience is unique. So, cast aside any of my thoughts on the subject which do not ring true or help you in some way.

> "NEVER COMPARE YOUR GRIEF.
> YOU – AND ONLY YOU – WALK YOUR PATH."
>
> **Nathalie Himmelrich**
> *Grieving Parents:*
> *Surviving Loss as a Couple*

My daughter Isabelle died, aged just 17, nine months after being diagnosed with cancer.

As a parent you tend to try to control many aspects of your child's life. When an event you cannot control, an illness or an accident takes them from you, it is devastating. The word "bereavement" comes from the ancient German for "seize by violence". When a child dies, it can feel just like that – as if your child has been ripped from you. The old English definition of "to bereave" is to "take a loved one from a person" or to "take something valuable or necessary from a person". The violence of the loss cannot be underestimated. The value of a child, their necessity to your life and to your happiness, means that their death deprives you of something fundamental and essential to your being.

Early days

The pain is almost unspeakable but at this most intense and private of times, life is inevitably busy. There are arrangements to be made, decisions to be taken and people to deal with, from medical professionals and funeral directors to family and friends.

One of the things I have read, and been told repeatedly, is that there are no rules for grieving. But, in fact, there are. There are conventions, traditions, accepted ways of behaving and of comforting the bereaved. They first appear in the making of arrangements in the hours, days and weeks following the loss of your child.

At times, having to deal with the necessary issues that arise may seem intrusive. The hard, cold arrangements that must be put in place may seem at odds with the enormous tidal wave of emotions you feel.

However, the need to make plans and be busy sorting out arrangements will get you through the first few awful days. Doctors and funeral directors, officials from religious organisations or perhaps humanist bodies, family and friends, will all be asking you to do things and to make decisions and, strangely, this will give you a focus.

You will find yourself feeling absolutely lost. The bottom has fallen out of your world. Every step feels like it could be over a cliff. The grief may feel almost like a physical pain. There has to be a way though. This can be as simple as getting up at a decent time every day, showering, getting dressed and sitting down to eat (whether you actually do eat or not) three meals a day. This is not going to bring them back, but it's how most people live so at least you'll be roughly in step with the world around you. Even though your world has stopped, the actual world of utility bills and grocery shopping keeps going with an almost rude disregard for the enormity of the pain you feel.

Sometimes it feels as if grief is attacking you. You will be almost floored by the strength of the emotion you feel. You may feel anxious or panicked or breathless. In addition, at times when you feel a bit calmer, you may feel anxious about another attack, another breakdown, about your ability to hold yourself together.

There are things that must be done

A doctor will need to certify the death.
I cannot easily describe the finality of this. It is too grim for words. Too sad. And wrong. And unnatural.

The death must be registered.
The death has to be registered within five days in England and Wales (eight days in Scotland). The registrar will give you the death certificate – as many copies as you request – and other documentation that you will need to organise the funeral.

Government buildings can be a bit drab and are often multifunctional over a bizarre range of things. Our local registry is – as they nearly all are – also a wedding venue. So, you are registering a death in a space designed for happy occasions. There was a laughably colourful riot of flowers in the flower beds outside where couples can pose for a life together, for better or worse. And we were in the middle of the worst.

The registrar was good. He commiserated us on our loss. Quietly and almost reverently, he explained the law and dealt with the formalities. And then we had to pay for the certificates and copies. I know government services have to be paid for, but it just seemed so vulgar. So commonplace. So transactional. And then it was over. And you drive home and it's official.

A funeral must be arranged.
Most people use a funeral director, though you can arrange a funeral yourself. Funerals do not have to be religious.

Isabelle had known she was dying for six to seven weeks and had been brave enough to tell us what she wanted. This was an enormous help to us. We felt we knew what we had to do and knowing that we were doing the right thing was a comfort. If you did not have this opportunity, you may intuitively know what to do and many people will be around to help. Follow your instinct – you knew your child best.

The funeral
Think about what feels right and be pretty selfish about creating it. It will turn out to be important that you did the right thing and that you gave your child the ceremony that was right for them. It will be of some comfort in the difficult weeks and months that follow. I have had the experience of a loved one not quite getting the send-off they deserved and, trust me, you do not need to heap guilt or regret on top of grief. It made me quite determined to make Isabelle's funeral as beautiful and as positive as she had been.

We chose to have a private family funeral followed by a service of thanksgiving for her life the next day. The funeral was unspeakably sad but saying goodbye just is. We lit candles in our beautiful local church with our closest family members. It was unbearably poignant, quietly beautiful and simple.

Then, just me, Mark and her sister went to the local crematorium. We rejoined the family for lunch. These ceremonies that have taken place for centuries, the traditions, the rituals like funerals and wakes, give you and all those friends and family who are mourning the loss some structure.

The service of thanksgiving was more informal. We were acutely conscious that Isabelle's friends needed to grieve but we wanted them to be able – in their own time – to move on, and so we wanted the service to be as positive as possible. We involved Isabelle's friends in the service, both to do the readings and to hand out orders of service. The advantage of having the funeral separately is that then there doesn't need to be a coffin at the thanksgiving/memorial service (important if there are other children in the congregation) and it can be more celebratory in tone. It may have been a short life, they may not have done many of the things they dreamt of doing, but all life is worth celebrating. Think of the positives – if nothing else, they made you happy. So, even if that is all you can think of, it is something worth celebrating.

This was the first reading at Isabelle's funeral:

> "WE CANNOT JUDGE A BIOGRAPHY BY ITS LENGTH, BY THE NUMBER OF PAGES IN IT; WE MUST JUDGE BY THE RICHNESS OF THE CONTENTS... SOMETIMES THE 'UNFINISHEDS' ARE AMONG THE MOST BEAUTIFUL SYMPHONIES."
>
> Victor Frankl
> **Men's Search for Meaning**

We were well advised by a super vicar who did not insist our daughter was taken by God to fulfil some master plan. He accepted her death was wrong and that helped. It was. To have pretended otherwise for convention would have simply added insult to injury. Our vicar encouraged us to choose music, songs and readings that were appropriate to a young person's funeral and that she would have wanted. It was probably the first time Taylor Swift was played in that church but it was exactly right. The vicar also encouraged us to choose a playlist of her favourite songs to be played as people arrived. It sets the tone. I would recommend it. (Check the lyrics, obviously.)

We put together an order of service full of pictures. This is quite common now and particularly important for a young person. When we were choosing pictures, we could not find one in which she was not smiling. It made us smile but it also brought home the enormity of our loss. At times the grief was almost overwhelming.

I heard a funeral director say of the family that they would spend the day of the funeral comforting people who were much less bereaved than them. How true. You will thank people for coming and tell them you are fine. This is, in part, because we all want to comfort other people. In part, it is simply a reflection of the fact the funeral is a ceremony, a formal and public occasion. It is not a reflection of the wee small hours in the morning when you are far from fine.

It is almost as if you are playing host. At times, you might feel that you are playing or acting, putting on a brave face. Do not feel bad or guilty about this. In a way, our ability to function at some level, even if only for short periods of time, is what gets us through.

If you do not have a religious figure who can guide you, you could ask a member of the British Humanist Association or a person who has been important in your child's life to help you with arrangements and officiate at the funeral. You can always write the eulogy yourself – as we did – even if you cannot deliver it.

Having said this, you will be in a state of shock and despair, so if you don't quite get it right you can always hold a memorial service or gathering of some type at a later date.

To those attending the funeral, it is important to remember that the bereaved parents are going to miss their child for the rest of their lives. You should not view the funeral as the end of something.

"There is no more ridiculous custom than the one that makes you express sympathy once and for all on a given day to a person whose sorrow will endure as long as his life. Such grief, felt in such a way is always present, it is never too late to talk about it, never repetitious to mention it again."

Marcel Proust

2

EARLY DAYS AFTER THE FUNERAL

Life has changed – fundamentally, drastically and forever.

When you lose a child, the grief is almost unbearably devastating. This loss, and coping with it, is a lifelong process. You never get over the death. All you can do is assimilate it and live with it. Inevitably, the early days will be full of cards and flowers and gifts of food and seemingly endless kindnesses. Nothing seems normal. Everything makes you cry. Assimilating anything seems unbelievable.

> "MOURNING IS THE CONSTANT RE-AWAKENING THAT THINGS ARE NOW DIFFERENT."
> **Stephanie Ericsson**

These are the strangest of days. You can't go back. You can't go forward. You probably can't sleep or eat or concentrate or stop thinking. All I can recommend is that you stick to the basics – get up, get clean, get dressed. If nothing else, sitting down to eat gives you a chance to check up on other members of the family.

I am reminded of the words of Samuel Beckett: "I can't go on, I'll go on."[1] I had to force myself to just keep going. The sadness was profound and the grief raw. Somehow you get through the day and the night and face another day. Being there when Isabelle died was truly awful. Being there afterwards has been worse.

Lack of guidance

There are supposedly five stages of grief: denial, anger, bargaining, depression and acceptance. However, many people think this is an oversimplification of the process of grieving and that the very individual nature of grief means that people will experience some or all of them, and not necessarily in a set order.

The idea of there being five stages of grief is based on observations made by Elisabeth Kübler-Ross, a Swiss-American psychiatrist, in *On Death and Dying* (1969)[2]. Kübler-Ross's five stages of loss and grief are:

Denial

One reaction to the death of a loved one is to deny the reality of the situation, which is a normal response to overwhelming emotions and acts as a defence mechanism to shield you from the immediate shock and to let you endure the pain.

Anger

This anger can be aimed at anyone or anything, from close friends or family to inanimate objects. It can be rational, such as blaming doctors for perceived incompetence, or irrational, such as anger at older people who have outlived your child. Anger may also be directed at the deceased – you may resent them for leaving you and causing you pain.

Bargaining

This is a normal response to feelings of helplessness. You feel the need to regain control and ask yourself if there was anything you could have done to change the inevitable.

Depression

Sadness about the death and missing the deceased.

Acceptance

Eventually, for most people, some form of acceptance is reached. You know and accept that your loved one has gone and cannot return. You begin to see beyond the events of the death and perceive the deceased's life as a whole. This final stage is supposedly marked by calm as the grief recedes. The bereaved may return to a more normal life.

To be fair to Kübler-Ross, she did not see these as set stages that people have to go through, nor did she suggest people go through them in a particular order. Over time, it seems that many writers have reduced her theory to a platitudinous list. She saw them more as aspects of bereavement, during which emotions would lurch unexpectedly from one to another. Pain would come in waves, but eventually it would subside.

As long as you do not expect to go through these different stages like some five-step recovery programme, her description is a useful guide to some of the experiences of bereavement that you might feel.

> "THE REALITY IS YOU WILL GRIEVE FOREVER.
> YOU WILL NOT 'GET OVER' THE LOSS OF A LOVED ONE;
> YOU WILL LEARN TO LIVE WITH IT.
> YOU WILL HEAL AND YOU WILL REBUILD YOURSELF
> AROUND THE LOSS YOU HAVE SUFFERED.
> YOU WILL BE WHOLE AGAIN BUT YOU WILL NEVER
> BE THE SAME AGAIN.
> NOR SHOULD YOU BE THE SAME, NOR SHOULD YOU WANT TO."
>
> **Elizabeth Kübler-Ross**

Recovery, I have concluded, is not possible. Recovery implies that you will get better and, although the quote above suggests you may heal, I suggest you will always be scarred. Recovery implies you will somehow get back to the way you were. Even if you wanted to, I doubt this would be possible. At best, all you can do is accept what has happened, adjust to life without your child and find a way of keeping their memory alive while you survive these early days as best you can.

Your bereavement will be unique. How you feel will change from day to day, hour to hour. You will be told that there is no correct way to grieve, no rule book, no timetable. So, whilst the "five-stage" labels might help psychologists and therapists and might give you some ability to articulate your feelings, what happens is that you find yourself in a great barren desert without road markings and without a map to negotiate them even if there were.

However, I think there are some general rules. There are, as already discussed, conventions and traditions which give some guidance and structure in the most bewildering of times. The Jewish faith, for example, has detailed provisions for different periods of mourning and sets out guidance as to how people should behave during each of those periods. The Muslim faith provides detailed guidance about the burial and mourning afterwards. Most faiths are diverse but, despite the gradual secularisation of society and the incredible body of knowledge we have gained from modern science, they still offer rituals and traditions that can guide and comfort the dying and the bereaved.

Also, I don't see why we can't make rules. Not hard, narrow or prescriptive rules, but general guidance to help not just people who have suffered a loss, but to help those trying to comfort them.

I have summarised some "rules" later, but here are some preliminary thoughts.

Crisis point
There is one hard and fast rule: if at any time you feel that you might harm yourself or others, get help.

Tell a friend or your doctor, call a help line. There are some numbers at the back of this book. The Samaritans are there for anyone at any time, 24 hours a day, seven days a week.

I think that even if you blurted it out to a complete stranger, they would help you. If you reach a point where you are at risk, tell someone, tell anyone.

You might not be able to imagine living another single day but the problem with grief is that it ebbs and flows, it creeps up on you, envelopes you and then it recedes. Get whatever help you need to get through the day because tomorrow you might feel differently. You won't necessarily feel better or feel better for any length of time, but how you feel will fluctuate.

Coping initially
It is immensely difficult in the early days just to keep going. To some extent – short of doing something dangerous or life-threatening – you should do whatever you need to do to get through those early days.

There will still be family and health professionals around at this stage, perhaps a vicar or other spiritual person, and they may be able to help. We decided not to take sleeping tablets but they may help you, or you may be offered other medication for anxiety or depression. Just do what you need to do.

One of the things that amazed me was that I was able to function quite normally, even if only for short periods of time. Grief allows you a few hours when you can do normal things: cook, eat a meal, watch TV, household chores.

Then, without warning, grief would overwhelm me. It still does.

I think it's good to cry. To howl and scream and sob. One of the great benefits of counselling for me was being given a safe space to just have a good cry. Strangely, I would feel better afterwards. I think it's important to say how you feel and be honest about how terrible the situation is. At times you cry anyway, even if you are trying not to.

> "EVEN IF YOU KNOW WHAT'S COMING,
> YOU'RE NEVER PREPARED FOR HOW IT FEELS."
> Natalie Standiford

The smallest of tasks can seem enormous and require extraordinary amounts of energy. You may also have to cope with no – or broken – sleep and a feeling of distraction or restlessness. At first you may have friends and family around to help you but eventually you may find that you have to tackle things on your own. You may make uncharacteristic mistakes and be much slower and more deliberate than before. I am not sure that it is a bad thing to just take things slowly. Do not expect too much of yourself.

You alone will know what you are capable of coping with and achieving. This is the one time people will accept you saying "no", so take advantage of this and if you don't want to do something, or just can't do something, say so.

Children are integral to who we are. We become parents and, to an extent, that defines us. After the death of a child, you will still be the parent of that child. Your child is not only woven into your identity but into the fabric of your life. Every time you set the table for three instead of four, you are reminded of their place in your family and the space their absence creates.

In this respect, in the early days, grief is like death by a thousand cuts. There are so many little things every day which will be different – you don't need to buy their favourite food, there will be one less towel in the bathroom. Tiny things will remind you of the enormity of your loss.

Saying goodbye

We were able to say goodbye to Isabelle – she was at home with us for the last seven weeks of her life. This was a deeply harrowing and intensely emotional period. What we said to her and her to us is deeply personal and intimate, and I do not intend to share it more than I have already in this book.

However, it occurs to me that people may not have had this privileged and special time. If you were not with your child or if things happened quickly in the period before their death, you may feel you have not had a proper opportunity to say goodbye or tell your child how much you love them.

The funeral may have given you this opportunity, but if you feel it was too public an event to say your own personal goodbyes, you might think about creating a chance for you to say goodbye yourself. This may be a few words – not even out loud – at the graveside or at the scattering of ashes. Or you may want to write things down, maybe a letter to your child. Or you may want to collect poems or pictures or articles that sum up how you feel about your child and allow you to articulate your goodbyes. If you lost a very young child, you might want to write a letter telling them all the hopes and dreams you had for them, all the things you wanted to do with them. It can be something you do at any stage, whenever you feel it is right.

Exercise/keeping busy
Grief is exhausting but it rarely lets you sleep through the night. And in the small hours of the morning, it is enormous, unconquerable, all-consuming. So, you often wake up tired and sometimes even more tired than when you went to bed. One advantage of exercise is that it physically exhausts you. It gives you a fighting

chance of some sleep. I am not suggesting triathlons. Gardening, cleaning – anything just to keep active.

Dog-walking saved me. Our English Pointer needs a good long walk every day and no matter how awful I felt, I got up, threw on the dog-walking clothes and headed out. I could rant away to myself or the dog about how I was feeling. I got some fresh air. Exercise is critical to sleep and general wellbeing and it forces you to get out of the house every day. It can be tempting to just stay in and avoid the world after such a momentous loss (discussed below).

So try to do something active. Ask family or friends to come out for a walk with you if you need company, even just for half an hour. Walk to a coffee shop, to the post box, to the end of your road. Or weed the garden. Wash the car. Don't worry about other people seeing you; you are doing it for yourself.

Agoraphobia

For many reasons, I felt it might be easier to never leave the house again. The world carries on regardless of your loss and the refusal of anything to change in the humdrum routine of life can seem anything from ridiculous to cruel.

People do their best but even the most well-meaning individual can say something to throw you off balance. One woman who I bumped into whilst out walking the dog suggested my daughter had lived no life at all. I am sure she meant it in the sense of it being unfair she had been taken so young, but I felt Isabelle did live a good happy life in which she had contributed and achieved much. As a result of her brief words I doubted my way of thinking. A short sentence led to spiralling thoughts and a few very sad days. But I remain convinced that people mean to help and if they say something clumsy, it is probably because when a child is terminally ill or dies suddenly there is nothing really to be said – not one single solitary thing will ever make anything right again. For all they will achieve, they might as well speak Swahili and offer you magic beans. But they are trying – they are reaching out as one human to another – and many, many more people say good things rather than bad.

There are hundreds of things out in the world that can remind you of the child you have lost and throw you off-kilter: a song, a glimpse of a school friend, their favourite restaurant, something they liked, or might have liked… but these hazards invade the home too. Just being at home, you will hear or see radio and television articles about a cure for cancer/a new asthma treatment/a road accident – whatever killed your child. Your home will be physically full of their things. There will be cards and flowers everywhere and these keep coming. You wouldn't want them to stop – the recognition of your trauma is important. You will need to deal with stuff – bank accounts, phones, etc. (See below – "practicalities").

Grief is something internal and therefore inescapable. You cannot avoid it, whether you stay in or venture out. Neither is right or wrong but in order to be able to carry on for yourself and for others, you do, at some point, have to get out into the world again. If you just can't face the world, consider asking a friend to come with you and do something unambitious – a quick coffee or a quick shop. Consider going slightly further afield than normal so that you reduce the risk of bumping into people you might know until you feel able to face them.

Plan your escape/ coping strategies
Before you go somewhere, to a social gathering or just the shops even, it might help you to plan an escape route. So, if you bump into someone at the petrol station or in a supermarket, you can control the situation if you start to feel you cannot cope. This can be as simple as saying "Must dash – running late – see you soon". Or, as you arrive for coffee or lunch or whatever, tell whoever you are meeting you can't stay long, that you have to get back for a delivery or for an appointment. Give yourself a way out. It might help you to feel that you only have to cope for as long as you feel able and that if you start to feel overwhelmed you can excuse yourself easily. Of course, with closer friends and family you can simply say that you don't feel great/strong/ready and that you need to go.

At work and when tackling more long-term commitments, you should perhaps consider how you want to deal with colleagues. You can say up-front whether you want to talk about your loss. Or you can plan a stock response to queries. This will give you the confidence to face work. You may notice people are awkward around you. The loss of a child is so very awful that an element of incomprehension and sadness will colour every interaction you have. Although time will not heal your grief (as discussed below), with time other people will relax around you, which, in turn, will make being with them easier for you.

Social media
Facebook is a particularly rich vein of sadness – mine it at your peril. The lovely (who wouldn't like them?) pictures of yet another gorgeous young thing going to a prom, passing their driving test, graduating, can be heart-rending. You can switch off and look the other way, so to speak, but wherever you look, there will be something else that could hurt you.

The difference is that although you will always see and hear things that might upset you, you can't necessarily avoid those things, whereas you can avoid social media. You don't need to go there. You may find the perfect lives portrayed there simply remind you of the loss you have suffered and the destruction wrought in your life.

Alternatively, you may use social media to convey information. It's a quick way to communicate with a large number of people. Or you may use it to find out what is going on and as a way of "joining" life again by taking an interest in the lives of others. If you find it makes you sad, you can always just stop dipping into that world for a while.

Unwanted touching – torture by a thousand hugs

I never worked out how to stop people hugging me when I really didn't want to be hugged. Maybe you will never have a day you don't want to be hugged. Occasionally I thought it would set me off and tears would follow, so I felt guarded and would have rather not had a hug. But most days it was a comfort. I feel like I've hugged everyone now. It will pass for you too and the hugs will stop. Humans want to give comfort. So, try to accept hugs and squeezes of the hand, arm etc, gracefully. It's kind of nice that people want to reach out.

Behave nicely

Grief is a feeling, a state of mind, an experience. It is not an excuse for bad behaviour. When Isabelle was really ill, I was often comforted by random acts of kindness by complete strangers. They could not have known what I was going through – they were just kind, thoroughly nice individuals – and they will never know how much their acts of kindness helped. So, similarly, even though grief has exhausted me and I carry that pain every day, I try to be kind. I don't know what battles other people face in their life. When we were out and about picking up things for our daughter in the last weeks of her life, people would not have known to look at us what we were going through. Kindness has once or twice been the thing that has stopped me going over the edge. So, I consciously force myself not to let my grief diminish me. I am not suggesting you go through life treating everyone as if they are nursing a dying child or are recently bereaved. But I am determined not to use my grief as an excuse. Try not to take out your anger and frustrations on other people – ultimately it will just make you feel bad.

Black humour

I remember when my father died, it was the first time I had ever met a funeral director or had any involvement with the organisation of a funeral. My father was 6'4". The funeral director was moving towards a discussion of the costs and fees involved, when suddenly he said, 'Your father was a very tall man', and for a minute I thought they charged for their services by the inch. I asked whether this would affect the cost and, quickly realising how ridiculous this was, we both laughed.

At another funeral, I thought I saw the brother-in-law of the deceased and stood up to embrace and kiss him. I did, in fact, kiss his twin brother, and again, the people I was with laughed.

At times even of the deepest grief, funny things happen. And even if laugh-out-loud moments don't catch you unawares, things will strike you as funny/inappropriate/bizarre.

When the funeral director turned up just after Isabelle had died, his assistant was wearing "Red or Dead" glasses. It seemed too ridiculous for words.

Don't feel bad for finding something funny in these difficult days. The feeling of slight hysteria following the death of your child will abate and it may be a long time before you actually laugh or find something amusing again. When you do start to enjoy things, guilt is inevitable, but a more positive way of looking at it is to accept laughter or pleasure as a way of defying death, of reclaiming the positive things your child brought into your life.

Feeling apologetic

Sometimes I have felt sorry for the people we have had to interact with – the registrar, the bank manager and so on. Third parties, if you like – not friends and family. These people were just going about their business and were dragged into our trauma. I have felt bad for being the harbinger of gloom.

To be fair, you just need to plod on and not worry about them, and, to the enormous credit of most of the professionals with whom we have dealt, they were just that – professional.

3

PRACTICALITIES – DEALING WITH THINGS AND SORTING THINGS OUT

I have read articles and interviews with parents who have lost their child suddenly in traumatic circumstances such as Hillsborough or terrorist attacks or abduction or violent crime. They keep their child's room just as it was, like a shrine. Fine. If that's what they need, that's just fine. If it helps them cope just one tiny iota, then that's just great.

Others will need to deal with the possessions left behind and, albeit screaming and howling and with a reluctance bearing on obsession, let go.

In sorting these things out, you are not denying the importance of your child or hiding them away or bringing them to an end. Death took them but they live on in your memory and your heart. Their spirit and the positive contribution they made to your life lives on. Just not in a pair of muddy football boots at the bottom of a cupboard.

> "DEATH LEAVES A HEARTACHE NO ONE CAN HEAL,
> LOVE LEAVES A MEMORY NO ONE CAN STEAL."
> **From a headstone in Ireland**

There will obviously be things you want to keep. There are no rules. (Again – there's a theme developing here.) You might put everything into one box or 20. You might choose a heavily decorated keepsake box or a big plastic crate. If in doubt, keep things – although I can't imagine ever having the strength to go back and whittle down the contents of the boxes…

We were always big givers to charity – the Oxfam "Bag It" scheme couldn't be easier and enables you to Gift Aid your donations of clothes and shoes. You may want to raise funds for a charity related to your child's death. I felt it helped me to know that old clothes and books might help someone else. Less of a waste, I thought, than that already wrought by the death of my child.

As part of recognising the importance of your child and the fact they live on in you, you might want to increase the number of or update the photographs of them in the house. Leave out any trophies they were awarded. Or make a memory picture box to keep. You should do whatever you need to do to enable you and your family to cope. If people don't want to sit in your lounge because there is a picture of your child there, that is their problem. They are only reminded of your unbearable loss for two minutes. You live with it every waking minute of the day and night. You are trying to remember them in a positive way. Other people need to man up.

> "I WOULD ALWAYS LOOK FOR CLUES TO HER IN BOOKS AND POEMS,
> I REALISED. I WOULD ALWAYS SEARCH FOR THE ECHOES OF THE LOST PERSON, THE SCRAPS OF WORDS AND BREATH, THE SILKEN TIES THAT SAY, LOOK: SHE EXISTED."
>
> Meghan O'Rourke
> Story's End

Things may need to be returned to your child's friends or to their school. If this is something you feel you cannot face, it is a job a friend could easily undertake. Or if you feel you must do it, perhaps ask someone to keep you company.

You may also want people to send you pictures of your child or share their memories of your child with you. Not having been asked, the prep school that Isabelle had attended (and that she loved) carefully reviewed their archives and sent us copies of all the pictures that they had of her. From sports days to school plays, we had a record of her time there. We were overwhelmed by such kindness. It is so important to you that other people remember your child that, even if you are still in the very early raw days of grief, I would recommend that you accept any offer to send you things that you receive.

Mobile phones and technology

Most children over a certain age will have computers or tablets or mobile phones. They will have created their own digital identity and you will need to deal with this, seeking help if you are not technologically or emotionally able to do so. You will need to:

Access your child's mobile phone, tablet or computer and online bank accounts. Isabelle gave us passwords and pin numbers before she died. With extraordinary resilience and practicality and grace, she thought through all the matters we would have to deal with and gave us all the information we might need. You may not have had the chance to do this and may need to contact service providers to access and protect your child's information. In relation to mobile phones, I found it incredibly sad to delete Isabelle's number from my phone. (Mark still hasn't.) I was never tempted to call her number to hear her voice (on her voicemail). However, I did not want there to be no audible record of her and did not want to delete her voice for all time. There is an online service that enables you to have their voicemail message recorded and save it before you cancel the account and I recommend this. It seems less final than deleting it forever and it's free.[3]

Back up and save online material and photographs from phones and computers. Your child will have hundreds of pictures you will not have seen from hundreds of events and places they went to without you.

Memorialise any Facebook pages. Consider posting a message first to contact your child's Facebook friends and allow them to post. Virtual mourning/commemoration may seem very alien to you but it is simply what young people do and if you can, you should allow them to grieve and say goodbye in this way. You may even find their words a comfort.

Bank accounts/savings accounts
Children under 18 (16 if they are in the armed forces) cannot make a will, and any assets that they have will be distributed under the rules of intestacy. In England and Wales and in Northern Ireland, this means that both the natural parents are equally entitled to the estate of the deceased. In Scotland, parents and siblings are entitled to the estate. In most cases, the estate of the child is likely to be quite small. But most older children will have bank accounts and some will have had savings accounts from birth. You will need to take copies of the death certificate, details of the account and proof of your identity and address. We found the banks we had to deal with to be most helpful and sympathetic. Most banks have departments to deal with deceased customers. If grandparents or others were making regular payments into any savings accounts, you will need to warn them you are closing the accounts.

Other issues

Older children may have driving licences, cars and National Insurance (NI) numbers. They may have been receiving benefits during any illness and you may have been receiving child benefit. The government run a "Tell Us Once" service which may help you deal with most of the technical issues, although not all areas offer the service. Where it is available, the registrar will probably advise you about it and give you a reference number you need to access the service.

You'll need the following details of the person who died:

* date of birth
* NI number
* driving licence number
* vehicle registration number
* passport number
* details of any benefits or entitlements they were getting (for example, personal independence payments)
* details of any local council services they were getting (for example, Blue Badge disabled parking)
* the name and address of their next of kin.
* Then the "Tell Us Once" service will contact:
* HM Revenue and Customs (HMRC) and Department for Work and Pensions (DWP) to deal with tax and cancel benefits

- ✻ The Passport Office – to cancel a British passport
- ✻ Driver and Vehicle Licensing Agency (DVLA) – to cancel a driving licence and to remove the person as the keeper of a vehicle
- ✻ the local council – to cancel a Blue Badge and remove the person from the electoral register.

Your child's possessions

In addition to saving and sorting through your child's physical possessions, you might want to consider giving some of them to other siblings or family members. Again, with extraordinary bravery and grace, Isabelle asked us to make sure her sister "inherited" some things. How and when you deal with this will depend not just on how you feel but on how other children in the family feel and are coping.

Back to work

If you work, you will have to go back to your place of work at some point. In an ideal world this would be when you think you are ready. However, the world is far from ideal and financial pressures or pressure from your employer may play a large part in when you go back.

You may go back to work earlier than other people think you should. If you need to be busy, to be back in a routine, just insist on going in, maybe on reduced hours or responsibilities if that is what you feel you need. Only you know what you need and what you are capable of doing. I worked part-time and irregularly from home. A friend (Lisa) was starting a new role setting up a shop and running it as shop manager. She told me she thought I was spending too much time at home and suggested I work a day a week in the shop with her. It was in a different town where no one knew me and it was something which I had not done before so it kept me busy, gave me routine and – to some extent – kept me going over the year I worked there. I needed to be busy. If you didn't work before losing your child and need something to keep you busy, when you are ready, think about work or volunteering. There are so many charities out there to which you could contribute.

4

GRIEF IS NOT A JOURNEY

Grief is not a journey. The modern tendency to describe everything as a journey is a bit mad, but in relation to grief it is just wrong.

You can't plan for it. There is no end to it. It's not life-enhancing. I have not at any stage felt I am travelling or moving through something. It does not have a smooth or predictable trajectory. At times, you will simply be side-swiped. I have heard these times described as "grief bursts". Sometimes, out of nowhere, a powerful surge of emotion will simply overwhelm you. The fear of this happening can be paralysing and I have failed to go to things because I felt I might not be able to control my emotions. At the end of the day people will understand, and I long ago lost any embarrassment at crying in public.

Neither do I feel grief is a "process" or something that must "run its course". It is not something to be "overcome". I reject any idea which suggests grief is a battle. This just sets you up for failure and is based on the – I think false – idea that it will come to an end at some point.

Some of this terminology comes from the fact that most of the grief that professionals, writers and others comment upon stems from the loss of an aged parent or a partner. The loss of a child or a young person or a middle-aged person is quite different. The loss of a child (whether you are burying a ten-year-old in your thirties or a 50-year-old in your seventies) is unnatural and rare. Of the 530,000 deaths registered in the UK in 2017, less than 6,000 were of children and young people under 25. Only 21,000 were of people aged between 25 and 50.[4]

I am not saying it is worse, nor am I in any way setting up a league table of grief. Grief is not a competition. When someone dies young – in their fifties even – it is just a fundamentally different experience than for most people experiencing bereavement because the family and friends of that individual effectively lose their future as well as their past. To bury a child of any age is not the expected course, not the natural order of things.

The ring theory of grief

As I have mentioned, you may find yourself – the most bereaved – comforting others less bereaved than yourself, especially at the funeral. It may happen at other times as people need you (and you may want) to give the lead and control social interactions.

However, more generally, and going forward after those initial days, the ring theory may help you and others know how to cope. When a bereavement occurs, it not only affects the immediate family but also the extended family, friends, the broader community where you live, your child's school community and beyond. If you imagine a series of concentric circles, those closest to the tragedy are in the middle of the first circle – the parents and siblings of the dead child. Then in the next circle are people closest to or related to those central people – the parents, siblings and other relatives of the bereaved parents. In the next circle are close friends. In the larger circles around the other circles are other friends, colleagues, more distant friends and members of the community, working outwards.

The ring theory then suggests rules as to how the people in the circles should behave. A person in the middle circle can cope any way he/she wants. The job of those in the larger circles is to listen and be supportive.

When talking to a person in a circle smaller than yours, remember that you are talking to someone closer to the tragedy. Your job is to help. You are not allowed to move your anger, fear or grief towards people in the circles smaller than yours. Express these emotions to those in your circle or outwards to larger circles. The concept is simple: "comfort *in*, dump *out*".

I would like to add some thoughts to this theory borne out of my own experience.

Your position in the cascade of circles is not determined by your title but by your actual relationship with the bereaved person in the middle. You may be a relative of the bereaved mother but live many miles away and have a relationship based on "high days and holidays". The bereaved mother may have a best friend to whom she is extraordinarily close. That friend has no specific familial title but will be in a circle closer to the centre than the relative.

I think the position in the circles is determined at the moment before tragedy strikes, before the accident or illness. The fact you were once very close to the bereaved but have lost touch means you will be in a larger circle than a very new friend who was very present in the recent life of the bereaved.

Bereavement does not enable anyone to move between circles. You cannot and should not race to the centre. You cannot and should not claim to be any closer to the bereaved than you actually are. Equally, man up – ideally you should not slink to the edges or outwards.

Lastly, I would say that whilst this theory is helpful, it is not to be taken too literally. Relationships are complicated. So, at points the lines of the circles may be blurry. Some people are particularly good at giving support even though they may be in a very distant circle. So long as they do not pretend to be more affected than they are, they can give comfort and support and you can accept this comfort and support, just as you would accept the comfort of strangers. Some people inevitably will not be able to provide the support you might expect of them given their position in the circles.

Also, not "dumping in" has its limits as a general rule. Sometimes you might want people to be honest about how they are feeling and not hide their feelings from you. You might want and need to know how your child's death has affected them. Sometimes you might want to hear about other people's worries so that you can be a good friend to them. You need to respect other people's realities. You might want to hear about their flat tyre or health worries just to be part of normal life. You might not want interactions to be about you all the time and you might want people to be honest with you rather than wrapping you up in cotton wool. I talk below about both respecting other people's grief and sympathising with them when they sweat the small stuff.

As time progressed, I found it oppressive that the focus was always on me. I wanted to hear about the outside world, what my friends were up to. I did, effectively, want people to "dump in".

Partly this is because, for me, grieving was an intensely private experience. The things we had gone through, particularly when we knew Isabelle was dying, were intimate and indescribable and I wanted to keep a lot of our experiences private. Partly this was because I needed not to be the centre of attention all the time. It's exhausting. Partly, I wanted to re-join the world, albeit in a limited way, and this required me to be there for others.

**Respect the grief of others,
especially your child's friends**

You are at the centre of the circle. However, it is important to remember all the others who are in mourning: relatives and your friends and, particularly when a young person dies, their friends. I know others are grieving – although I am not sure I can help much other than to keep plodding on and hope they find the strength to do so too.

As a family we have been overwhelmed by the generosity, maturity and kindness of Isabelle's friends. They have been brave enough to stay in touch and write to us and remember her on her birthday. They have organised fundraisers and I was told they wanted her to be included in the school yearbook. They have acknowledged her absence from events she would have taken part in. Despite busy lives, they have taken time to honour her memory. They have shown honesty and kindness where, frankly, some adults have been lacking. I have immense affection and respect for them. I know they miss her and I hope they can take something positive from her death, even if it is just to go forward and wring every last ounce of joy out of life.

In an email, a friend mentions in passing that she and her daughter – one of Isabelle's closest friends – often think of Isabelle. I thank her for remembering Isabelle. She replies: "Isabelle is never, ever forgotten & ***** & I continually share the enriching experiences we had with

Isabelle." I am humbled on two counts. First, it reminds me that others miss her and grieve her loss. Secondly, I am grateful for her positive comment. Sometimes this is all it takes to support a bereaved person – a kind word.

So Isabelle's friends grieve for her too. They had a relationship with her quite independent of her relationship with her family. This is a further caveat to the ring theory of grief. Many people may be affected by your child's death and you need to recognise your child had relationships in which you played no part. This will especially true the older the child is.

Although your child's life was shorter than it should have been, they may have achieved much and they will have touched many.

Grief turns the volume up

I have heard death described as "the great exposer" – exposing the strengths and weaknesses in people and relationships. I think this is true to some extent.

I found that what we were going through did not change people around us, but it did amplify their behaviour both in a positive and negative way. People who were good friends and good at dealing with things, people who had always been the type of person to do or say the right thing, were brilliant. Tiny gestures and kindnesses seemed so much greater and more important. People who had never been brilliant, and who had been disappointing in the past, were again, and their silly comments and failure to step up seemed so much worse. In many ways, it has made us less tolerant of some of the people in our lives for whom we have always made excuses.

The experience has reminded me of coming out of hospital after Isabelle was born. Having been in an idyllic bubble of new motherhood for days, I remember coming out into the world and being overwhelmed by it – it seemed so noisy, fast, busy. Grief seems to have this affect. It magnifies things. It turns the volume up.

To some extent this is part of a process whereby your priorities might change. We have never hankered after a Caribbean holiday home or a yacht or a swimming pool. We have always put family first and taken pleasure in the little things. It is not as if we needed to be taught a lesson. Losing Isabelle has not made us re-evaluate our lives. And discovering we were right all along to prioritise family and enjoy simple things has given us no joy. However, we do feel differently – inevitably – about the future, about who and what is important to us. It has confirmed, I think, what we value and made us less tolerant (again, inevitably, but perhaps also sadly) of people who have, and do, let us down.

I find the hardest people to deal with are those who weren't great before Isabelle became ill. Those who forgot her birthday or let her down. A friend suggests I am channelling my anger at these people. I am not sure this is right. I am not angry with them. If anything, I am just tired of them.

I read somewhere that "grief reorganises your address book". Some friendships will not survive the shift in your outlook and priorities. There is no need for any confrontation. I am not sure it is even a bad thing to re-evaluate what is and who is important to you. You will simply invest in those who invested in you and your child. Some of my friends have gone above and beyond to look after me and, when Isabelle was ill, to look after her and our family. These friendships have been strengthened. I cannot imagine my life without them in it. The "reorganisation of the address book" does not have to be a negative thing.

On the whole, most people have been amazing. In the face of a rare and desperately sad tragedy which no one in their right mind would have expected, people have been kind and thoughtful. We are constantly reminded of our loss but equally, we are constantly comforted by others. You will find this – there will be flowers and cottage pie left on your doorstep, kind words, quick hugs.

Giving and receiving advice

Before you tell someone who has lost a child about how to cope with the loss, think, "Have I lost a child?" If not, tread carefully. Unless you are prepared to take a call at 3am, you will have no idea of the abyss of grief the bereaved stares into in the wee small hours of the morning.

> "WELL, EVERYONE CAN MASTER A GRIEF BUT HE THAT HAS IT."
>
> William Shakespeare

Even if you have been bereaved, circumstances, experience and reactions are unique. All loss is valid. But it's not the same. Telling someone who has just buried a child that you know what they are going through is unlikely to be helpful. Yes, you may have suffered a loss, but it is not the same and you have no right to comment on, and little experience of what it is actually like to hold your child as they take their last breath.

However, whilst you cannot cure the bereaved, you can be there.

You can be there, you can listen, you can be present. You can ensure the bereaved knows you are around. After Isabelle's diagnosis, a mother from her school to whom I was not particularly close and who did not live nearby approached me at a school event. She looked me in the eye and said that she could not be of any practical help to me whatsoever, but she wanted me to know she thought about me every minute of every day. That was an enormous comfort.

After Isabelle's death, all sorts of people left food on the doorstep and flowers and notes and gifts. People sent texts and emails. After they had got over the initial shock, people began to tell us how much Isabelle had meant to them. Of course, there are always exceptions. One lady scrabbled up the steep bank of a valley to avoid us when she saw us walking towards her. A couple of times in the supermarket, acquaintances veered back round into the next aisle rather than bump into me. I did not let this upset me. It is really hard to know what to say and I accept they may have simply not had the words. What is important is that if you actually do meet someone who has been bereaved, you do find the words. It is really important that you do acknowledge the loss. This is true even months later – if it is the first time you have met with the bereaved, you must acknowledge the loss. Just as you would congratulate someone on their recent engagement or on having a child or getting a new job, it is important to acknowledge the change in their circumstances. You can keep it brief and change the subject fairly briskly if you want to, but please do say something. We found it bewildering when people ignored our loss and comforting when they mentioned it. We do not want Isabelle and our loss of her to be ignored.

Once you are strong enough to be out and about you will meet people who offer advice and who want to share their experiences with you. If you feel that putting one foot in front of the other is a tip-top achievement for the day, the well-meant but often misguided advice of someone else will be difficult to receive gracefully. Remember, first, they have no idea what you are going through; second, they mean well; third, they are a victim of there being no rule book; and fourth, it would be a grim, lonely and isolated world if no one spoke to you at all. So you might have to accept some clumsiness as the price for reintegration with the world.

This situation is more complicated when those around you are also bereaved by your loss. Your mum has lost a grandchild and sees you in pain. Your sister-in-law has lost a niece. Remember, grief is like ripples on a pond – it spreads out, touching many people as it goes. You are at its epicenter, but many others will be affected and their grief is equally valid and, indeed, may be greater or less than their place in the ripples. People right on the outskirts of your life can be profoundly affected by the death of your child. (See section on ring theory above.) Everyone has their own reality. Try to respect it.

There is no place for the word "should". If you are bereaved there is nothing you "should" do – just do what is right for you. For friends, never start a sentence with the words "you should". The one thing that should never happen has happened, and there is nothing the bereaved should do other than carve out a life in the shadow of the grief that will live with them forever.

Advice to friends of the bereaved

Read the sections above on the ring theory of grief and giving advice.

Accept that you cannot fix this. It is a perfectly natural response to want to make things right but accept quickly that you just can't make good the loss of a child. There are lots of things you can do but it is important to accept you cannot take away your friend's loss.

You may not be the centre of your friend's world for a bit. The bereaved may not be able to give anything to anyone for a while and you may just need to accept that your relationship is a bit one-sided for a time.

Be reliable. If you say you are going to do something or be somewhere, don't let a bereaved person down. They may be having a bad day and you letting them down may upset them disproportionately. On bad days, the smallest of things could send them over the edge.

No gossip. Your friend's loss, and their grief, is not for whispered conversations with all and sundry and is not to be belittled or exaggerated. Of course, you will talk about it, but be respectful and honest. Don't try to score points with "news" or allow other people to cajole you to disclose more information than you feel comfortable with. I recall one friend simply saying that her friend was dealing with the loss of her husband 'with great dignity'. I felt she was being honest and loyal and it was a clever way of stopping any further prying on that occasion.

Man up, if asked. If you are asked to accompany the bereaved on a particular task, do try and help. If you would really be useless, just say so and suggest another friend. But if your friend feels strong enough to, for example, donate some of her deceased child's clothes, you should find the strength to help. They are dealing with the belongings of their beloved child, things bought with love and hope and expectation. You are dealing with a few plastic bags. Be sensitive but strong, if asked.

Just be there. Call, leave messages, offer support. If you can, don't just say "call me when you are ready" but call them; leave things on the doorstep; make arrangements to pick them up, collect them, help. Hard arrangements, not vague promises. Although to be honest, vague promises and open-ended arrangements are better than nothing and are still a comfort.

In this digital world it takes little time, and not much more effort, to send an email or text. You can easily just say "thinking of you" and maintain contact. You can offer dates – not just coffee "some time", but coffee next week, Tuesday or Thursday? If the bereaved feels up to coffee they can accept the offer and, if not, they can refuse it. Try to encourage them to come to you rather than dropping in on them.

Social life
Social gatherings are tough at first. You will face a succession of well-meant questions over and over. It's like being at a grief speed-dating event. The hardest thing is seeing people for the first time, especially acquaintances rather than close friends, who ask after you and your family. But it has to be done – you need at some point to function in the wider world. The second and third time

you meet people, and all subsequent occasions, will be easier once you get over these initial enquiries.

Moreover, as I have said above, it is so much better for people to acknowledge your loss than to ignore it. You have been through and are struggling with the most extraordinary tragedy and it is right and respectful that this is acknowledged.

One or two friends will be the people with whom you can really share how you are feeling. It is important, I think, that you can also talk to them about other things, either at your request to have some "time off" or to protect them from always experiencing your grief. Also, if all you ever talk about is your grief, you will become even more isolated – you will not hear other people's news, life will pass you by and you will continue to feel on the outside of things.

Frustration
It is not unnatural to feel frustration with other people being rubbish and aspects of life not going smoothly. Sometimes people are rubbish – not in the context of your grief, just in everyday life. Sometimes, things just don't work.

I couldn't believe that my daughter, who had so embraced life and who had put so much effort into things, who had been so energetic and enthusiastic about everything, had had her life taken away – whilst others, who still had their lives, were carrying on with so little effort or enthusiasm, or were doing dreadful things to other human beings.

Experts have told me that guilt is the most damaging of emotions and has no place in grief. If people do irritate you, don't feel bad about it – just don't take it out on them (see "Behave nicely" in Chapter Two). You would have been frustrated even if you hadn't been bereaved. Sometimes life is just hard, so don't beat yourself up if you feel impatient or irritated.

Quite quickly I realised that many little things that would have annoyed me in the past simply didn't matter. I wonder if this could go too far? If you find yourself not caring about anything at all, you may need to talk to someone. I think depression (when you may feel empty and numb) is different from grief (when you feel the pain of loss). It is also similar, as in both cases you may feel completely and utterly helpless and hopeless. If you stop caring about anything, you may be suffering from depression. Tell your GP – there is help out there.

Comforting others

It is amazing how many times, from the funeral onwards, you will find yourself comforting others. I did not resent this at all, although it did occasionally exhaust me. You wonder how you can find the words, the energy to comfort others. But you will. It is a role you will find yourself in and you will surprise yourself. It is such a basic human desire to reach out to another, that's what you will instinctively do. You yourself will know the days you are not able to cope and then you need a tactic to deal with others needing comfort.

You will need to find your own way, but these are my thoughts:

Do not shy away from people.

Isolation is not a solution. Ultimately, loneliness will only add to your sadness. Although time will never heal the loss you feel, in time others will talk to you less and less about your situation.

Try changing the subject.

Try to control the conversation if you need to steer it away from you. If that doesn't work, be explicit – say, "Do you mind if we don't talk about this today?"

Avoid sitting still.

Walk the dog with friends or go to a neutral territory – a cafe or shop. At work, head for the coffee machine. Do not allow yourself to be physically penned in if you cannot face any interaction that might follow.

Have time limits or exit strategies.

Prepare a strategy so that you can cut difficult situations short. Just say: "Oh, must go…" that your parking expires; you must collect something/someone; you have work, supper, shopping, ironing to do.

Making mistakes
You will not always know what to do, nor will you always do the right thing. Grief, especially in the early days, can cloud your judgement. You are changed by your experience, and bereavement is not only about mourning the loss of your child but also the loss of the old you. It may take some time to come to accept the new you and understand your limitations.

If you do misjudge things in the early days, just accept it. Go easy on yourself. Do not feel that if you do get something wrong, you have let your child down. Nothing you do will change your love for the person who died. Nothing will diminish your love for the child you lost.

Sympathising with others sweating the small stuff
A friend whose day is ruined by a missed train has still had a really rough day. It's not big in the grand scheme of things but it's still her reality and she's entitled to feel low and complain if she wants. You might want to scream, "Oh, just get over it", but you must respect her feelings as they are totally valid.

You would not want people to hide things from you for fear of seeming ungrateful or insignificant – otherwise everyone around you will be falsely happy all the time, failing to complain or to be honest with you because your position is, and forever will be, worse than theirs. It would be like being surrounded by a million Pollyannas. You would go mad.

5

COUNSELLING

I was advised to arrange counselling for Isabelle's sister while Isabelle was ill and this turned out to be very good advice (thank you, Carol). Before Isabelle died, her sister was already seeing – and had established a relationship with – a counsellor and this proved invaluable when she had to face the death of her sister.

I sought counselling from the same organisation and was lucky to receive a few sessions, but for many people counselling is not available or there is a long waiting list.

In this country, counselling provision in the event of bereavement is poor. This is not surprising. There are so many deserving causes and resources are necessarily spread thinly. The Cruse Bereavement Care Annual Report 2014/15 noted that: *"In 2014, 501,424 people died in the UK leaving between two and three million bereaved mothers, sisters, husbands, brothers, wives, daughters, fathers, uncles, nephews, grandmothers, aunts, sons, grandfathers, partners, nieces, cousins, colleagues and friends."* That means a lot of people are affected by a bereavement every year.

According to the 2014 survey carried out by the We Need to Talk Coalition[5], out of 2,000 people who tried to access talking therapies in 2014, only 15% were offered the full range recommended by the National Institute for Health and Care Excellence (NICE). That means a high percentage of people affected by bereavement were unable to access talking therapies. If you think it would help you to talk to an expert, push for it. There are some numbers at the back of this book of organisations that might be able to help. Some provide telephone help, some group sessions, some information. If you are not strong enough to fight for the help you feel you need, pick a determined friend and ask them to find help for you.

I found it a tremendous relief to talk to a stranger about how I was feeling. I found I could say how I felt without burdening a friend. I felt safe.

Of all deaths registered in any year, only 1.2% will be of children and young people under 25 years. To lose a child is rare. It is a particularly awful and devastating loss, and it is in no way an admission of weakness to seek help.

I started this book as a journal when Isabelle was in hospital. At the time, Isabelle was blogging about her experiences as a teenager with cancer, how she was coping with hair loss and all the procedures and treatments. She wanted to reach out to children and other young people. Her blog, Izzy D Cancer Is Not Me, ultimately became linked to her JustGiving page.[6] She had not intended to raise funds but a complete stranger read one of her blogs and asked if he could donate. At the time of publication, her JustGiving page to raise funds for Teenage Cancer Trust stands at £32,500; another £37,500 has been donated separately to the Teenage Cancer Trust in her memory, and a further £6,000 donated to the Little Princess Trust, which provides wigs to young people who have lost their hair as a result of chemotherapy or other drug treatments. The proceeds of this book will add to these figures.

I wrote down how I was feeling to try and make sense of what was happening to Isabelle and to our family. It helped. So, if you can't get counselling or think it might not be for you, or if you do not feel ready for it, you might consider a journal or blog or just scribbling down some thoughts.

Counselling can take different forms. Counselling is available on a one-on-one basis or in groups. The counsellor will not try to provide an answer but will allow you to discuss your emotions. The counsellor should set out the basis of your meetings – how many sessions are involved, how long they last, how privacy and confidentiality is maintained. The counsellor will give you a safe space to talk about the child you have lost and will help you think things through and develop coping strategies. It is normal and perfectly acceptable to cry during sessions. Indeed, I found it impossible not to cry.

> "THERE IS A SACREDNESS IN TEARS. THEY ARE NOT THE MARK OF WEAKNESS, BUT OF POWER. THEY SPEAK MORE ELOQUENTLY THAN TEN THOUSAND TONGUES. THEY ARE THE MESSENGERS OF OVERWHELMING GRIEF, OF DEEP CONTRITION, AND OF UNSPEAKABLE LOVE."
>
> **Washington Irving**

In addition, there are support groups. In so many other areas of life, we talk about how we feel with people in the same situation as us. I am not sure why bereavement should be any different. There are even online forums and podcasts. Gaining support and knowledge from others is something to consider.

It might be that a particular friend – or different friends on different occasions – is the person you choose to talk to and who can support you. It might be that you talk to a partner.

There are helplines if you can't bear talking to someone face to face or if you need to talk to someone urgently.

In relation to talking about grief, I would suggest "better out than in", although Shakespeare says it rather better:

> "THE GRIEF THAT DOES NOT SPEAK WHISPERS THE O'ERFRAUGHT HEART AND BIDS IT BREAK"
>
> **William Shakespeare**

In an ideal world, you will find someone who listens, lets you talk about whatever you need to discuss and accepts you as you are. Obviously, professionals have the edge here and if you can find a counsellor who can help that's great. However, a really good friend or a support group can work equally well and, to some extent, you need to try different options until you find something that helps, if you need help.

Articulating your feelings is difficult but helps you to identify what you are actually feeling. You can always just talk to yourself or write things down to sort out in your head what you are feeling.

Being fine

In the early days, when anyone asked me how I was, I would say that I was fine. One day a friend said: "Really? Are you *really* fine?"

"Fine" is short for: "Well, I managed to get up and get dressed in clean clothes and do the stuff that needed to be done and got my child to school and walked the dog and I am here and not sitting at home weeping and I am putting one foot in front of the other and managing and today is okay and I have slept a bit more but still have nights when I don't sleep at all and am so full of despair I can't believe I wake up in the morning and I have days I am so sad it is impossible to explain and there seems to be no end to the things that upset me like just the other day I was packing away a coat of Isabelle's and I found a whole packet of painkillers and it reminded me of the pain she went through and the effort she put in to going to school between chemotherapy sessions and trying to have a normal life and bearing in mind how brave she was I am trying to soldier on but it is exhausting and I really miss her and the way she used to dance around the kitchen and hug me and tell me her news and the way she was so enthusiastic about things and I can't believe this has happened to our little family and I am worried about Mark and her sister and dreading the memorial service/speech day/whatever next week and I am bowled over by people's kindness and how much they cared about her and they thought she was special too which is great but it also makes me feel our loss more keenly and we are just devastated but functioning, you know?"

So probably best, when you bump into someone in the street, just to accept "Fine". Sometimes it is appropriate to talk about your loss and have a good cry, but sometimes you just need to be allowed to cope and muddle through.

6

LIVING WITH GRIEF

Some people view grief as a challenge, something to get through. Others view it as an enemy. I have come to the view that grief is just something I am going to have to live with for the rest of my life. Somehow, I have to accommodate it and get on with my life with the all-pervading presence of grief and sorrow. So, I don't wish it away – I think this would be futile and exhausting and would ultimately fail. I don't rail against it – I accept it as the price of the love I felt for my daughter. I sort of rub along with it. The words that spring to mind are: "Hello darkness, my old friend".[7]

This is not a negative standpoint. It's not that I have given in, but just accepting the pain makes it somehow easier to bear. And recognising that you will always miss your child is just the truth. It would belittle your loss and their unique position in your heart to think you could ever get over the loss. But living positively with the loss is the balancing act you need to achieve. It will ebb and flow but it will never disappear. All sorts of people carry all sorts of scars from loss or experience or mental health problems. Your grief is your scar.

Ken Loach, the film producer who lost a son in a car crash, when interviewed by Becky Millican described living with his loss as having "a stone in your heart". He described carrying it with him every day and thinking about it every day. He also noted how it informs your understanding of the loss suffered by others.[8]

It is isolating carrying this darkness. You may always feel some distance from those around you, from your old life and, indeed, your old self.

> "JUST AS IT IS IMPOSSIBLE TO EXPLAIN CHILDBIRTH TO A WOMAN WHO HAS NEVER GIVEN BIRTH, IT IS IMPOSSIBLE TO EXPLAIN CHILD LOSS TO A PERSON WHO HAS NEVER LOST A CHILD."
>
> Lynda Chedelin Fell

Big days – anniversaries, birthdays, Christmas

Something to remember – it's just a day. The funeral. Their birthday. The first Christmas. Mother's Day. Father's Day. They are just days. Single days. Painful days. But you are going to miss your child for the rest of your life so unless it helps, there is not much point getting too upset on any particular day. Maybe you feel they are a useful focus for your grief and maybe marking a special date might help you. This is good. But I remember thinking, when people asked how

I'd got through the funeral, that I was a lot more worried about how I'd get through the next 20 years. The funeral is similar to a wedding, and not just because you can do them both in thickly carpeted government buildings. Like a wedding, it is at the time an incredibly important ceremony into which much effort and thought and expense is poured. But it's just one day. And as with a good marriage, it's the days, weeks, months and years afterwards that need to be negotiated.

I find birthdays and other significant dates hard – like particularly high waves in an ocean of grief. I feel that they are days I have to get through or survive but I know I also have to negotiate many other days. A grey Wednesday in February with no special significance can be as hard to get through as a particular special date or anniversary. Grief has no respect for time or dates. It ambushes you at the strangest of times.

> "HERE IS ONE OF THE WORST THINGS ABOUT HAVING SOMEONE YOU LOVE DIE: IT HAPPENS AGAIN EVERY SINGLE MORNING."
>
> Anna Quidlen

Grief never has a day off. Every morning you have to face the reality of your loss. Some days will be harder than others. You may feel better for days and then suddenly – perhaps inexplicably – worse for days. The sheer unremitting nature of grief may wear you down so that you find it harder to cope as time goes on.

Because Isabelle was ill, she had time to talk to us about how she felt. It was heart-rending. But at least we were able to tell her how deeply and absolutely she was loved. We know from those conversations that she was scared that she would be forgotten and that her death would ruin our lives. Of course, we will never forget Isabelle.

> "AS LONG AS WE LIVE, THEY TOO WILL LIVE;
> FOR THEY ARE NOW A PART OF US;
> AS WE REMEMBER THEM."
>
> Jewish Prayer

It is hard, though, to watch her friends and our friends move on. Of course, they must move on and we do not want anyone else to struggle or suffer. But we do not want her memory to fade. We have donated a bench to her old school engraved with her name and we have donated a cup in her name to her school cadet force (which she loved). Maybe a birthday or anniversary or other important date is a good time to do something to keep the memory of your child alive. Plant a tree or a rose, name a star, light a candle – whatever you think might help you.

As well as remembering your child, you may want, or indeed need, something good to come out of their death, as a way of making their short life matter. You don't have to make a grand gesture or raise pots of money. You might equally touch the life of someone else by donating a box of toys to a hospital (embossed with your child's name if you want) or equipment to a paediatric unit.

Isabelle endured (palliative) radiotherapy. As we waited beside the aquarium in the dedicated children's waiting area, we often heard smaller children crying as they were held still and tight to the treatment tables by casts or masks. In her last days, she ordered a print of Dory telling Nemo[9] to "Just Keep Swimming" and sent it to the radiotherapy department, where they have put it up in that waiting area. It was her message of hope to other children. Maybe you could do something in your child's memory that might give hope to others.

As for her death ruining our lives – well, although we tried to reassure her, our lives were changed forever and fundamentally the minute we knew she was going to die. We will forge a way forward but we are devastated.

At every birthday, Christmas and other anniversary we will think of her. But then we do every day.

A friend, who lost her son aged 15, told me things would get easier after the first year. The loss would not get any less or any easier to bear but, having got through that first year of firsts – the first birthday, the first Christmas, the first anniversary of the death – you would know you had survived. This alone would enable you to face the next year and the next round of anniversaries, significant dates and other events. It might be that certain days are harder in the second or third year, but the knowledge that you have got this far may help you go further.

Complicated grief and post-traumatic stress (PTS)

I have concluded that you never get over the death of a child, but most people get back to work and at least a semblance of normal life. However, there is research[10] which suggests a small percentage of people experience chronic and disabling grief and sometimes PTS. Symptoms of PTS may include nightmares, flashbacks or frequent intrusive thoughts about the circumstances of the loss.

PTS symptoms are more common when the death was caused by violence, such as a physical attack or during military service, or a stigmatising loss, such as suicide. PTS is also more common when a child dies in hospital or in intensive care rather than at home or in a hospice, when parents care for a terminally ill child for long periods, or when parents had no time to prepare for their child's death.

We stayed with Isabelle at the Teenage Cancer Trust (TCT) Unit at University College Hospital (UCH) for all of the chemotherapy sessions and all her other treatments. One of the great things about a TCT Unit is that every hospital bed has a fold-out bed for relatives, and parents are actively encouraged to stay on the ward. Some of the procedures and treatments she had to go through were brutal. At the end of the day, despite the expertise of doctors, the super nursing staff and the scientists in laboratories all over the world, the current chemotherapy regimes involve pumping the body full of poison. We were with her for endoscopies, biopsies, radiotherapy and endless other procedures and appointments. We saw children on the ward endure amputations, operations and terrible side effects from tough drug regimes, and we saw families broken by bad news. It was traumatic. The fact that in some parts of the country some young people have to go through such things on adult wards is why Isabelle wanted to raise funds for the TCT. If your child died of an illness or in an accident or at the hands of another person, it will have been traumatic. Images and flashbacks may cloud your thoughts. If this becomes unbearable or affects your ability to function, you will need professional help. There has been much discussion recently of mental health and there is no sense of failure if you admit you are not coping.

If (and I cannot repeat this enough) you might harm yourself or anyone else – tell someone.

Telling strangers

I had decided, if asked how many children I had, to say two and explain that one had died. To do otherwise felt wrong. However, the first time it happened, I did not keep my promise to myself. Isabelle had asked that at the thanksgiving service to celebrate her life, everyone wear bright colours. Her sister needed a brightly coloured dress, so we went shopping. The assistant staffing the changing rooms admired her when she came out of the changing room to show us one of her choices. "Is it for her prom?" she asked. "No," we said. "Is she your only one?" she asked. I sort of nodded uncommittedly. It seemed wrong to upset her or make her feel uncomfortable by saying no, she wasn't our only daughter, our first had died and the dress was for her funeral. But equally it seemed so wrong not to have told the truth.

Subsequently, I have found the strength to explain that I had two children but lost one to cancer and move the conversation on. It's probably best to think in advance how you want to answer this question if it comes up and work out some words with which you feel comfortable.

Guilt

You can feel guilty for everything from living on to having fun. It's such a negative emotion, but the most natural. It is something niggling away at the back of your mind unbidden.

I have mentioned above how I have been told guilt has no place in grief. However, I am not sure you can escape it completely. If your child was ill, you might feel guilty that you didn't notice the symptoms earlier. If your child died in an accident, you may feel guilty for not being there, or for being there but surviving. You might feel guilty for feeling relieved that your child's suffering is over.

Guilt is intensely personal because it flows from your unique view of the world and what you believe about yourself and about what is morally right. If you feel you have to admit to yourself that you have breached your own moral code or fallen short of the behaviour you would have liked to exhibit, do so. Then move on. Guilt nearly always flows from being unable to change a situation – or else you would make those changes to escape the guilt, if possible. So as you are unable to change the situation, let the guilt go. If you can't, this might be something to discuss with a counsellor. It's a negative, gnawing emotion.

In many respects we were lucky, in that we were given permission by Isabelle to enjoy life. She wrote:

> *"I want to be remembered as I was when I was healthy, and full of life. Please take the positive memories of me and remember them – I would never want any of you to get upset over this, I want you to be happy and live your lives.*
>
> *Speaking of such, cancer has taught me to treasure every minute. You don't need me to tell you that life can be short, so try and find a moment to treasure every day, not for me but for you. It's okay for life to be short if you fill it with good times."*

Life is not what you thought

As the death of a child defies the expected natural order of life events, many parents feel their fundamental understanding of life is blown apart. You had a rough idea of how your life was going and what the future held, and this has been ripped from you.

Things you might have thought important in the past, ambitions you may have had or hobbies, might suddenly seem irrelevant. You may feel that nothing matters. You may question some of the things you thought in the past and you may feel ambivalent about the future.

> "IT'S SO MUCH DARKER WHEN A LIGHT GOES OUT THAN IT WOULD HAVE BEEN IF IT HAD NEVER SHONE."
>
> John Steinbeck

I agree with Steinbeck in one sense – the darkness, the loss, is all encompassing. However, I have come to believe that I would rather go through this pain and have had Isabelle in my life than not have had her at all. HM Queen Elizabeth II famously said that pain is the price we pay for love. Life will never be the same, nor should it be, and we are forever changed by the grief we feel. But you can hold the light that your child brought into your life inside you and, although the things that mattered before might never feel as important again, you can find a way to live.

A child carries their parents' emotions, fears, joys and hopes for the future. Once a child is gone, that part of a parent is also gone forever. Your plans for the future, your hopes and dreams, are gone. You may not have had any particularly large plans (we didn't) but in a way, the hardest thing is losing the very ordinary future you imagined.

Some people think that the past is also damaged – all those sleepless nights, school runs, music lessons, birthday parties, costumes for school, family traditions and private jokes, all that love poured into someone who is now gone. I think, in time, the past will provide many happy memories. Not one day was wasted, not one broken night was lost. In time, you will look back and smile.

The world is ugly/the world is beautiful

It is hard not to look at the world and be disappointed by it. After something so shocking, so momentous, so life-changing, you expect life to be different. The occasional dullness and minor irritations of ordinary life remain.

On other days, the blueness of the sky or the colour of the leaves or a piece of music will shock you with its beauty.

Just as the mundane tasks of life carry on regardless of your grief, nature rolls out the seasons with scant regard to your misery. I recently heard an interview with former PM John Major, who admitted that the

Warrington bomb had reduced him to tears. He was walking round the garden at Chequers looking at the daffodils when the phone rang to tell him that two little boys had been killed. He thought it might end the peace process but although promises had been broken, he decided to persevere. Otherwise, more little boys would be killed by bombs. And whether wrong or right, the daffodils would come up the next year and every year after that.

The snowdrops will flower, the bluebells will carpet the ground, the daffodils will bloom, leaves will fall. There is an inevitability to the passage of time. This certainty can be a comfort when your understanding of the world has been turned on its head. It is also sad to think how many seasons will pass without your child in the world.

As I have said, for some considerable time after Isabelle's death everything seemed – and still now seems – slightly amplified. I still feel things more sharply than I did before. I do not know if this is normal, this strange over-sensitivity. I just accept it as one of the many things that have changed in my life.

I have always – for such a strong person – been sentimental. I can feel my eyes prick with tears at a sad film or news story. Now it's much worse. It seems ridiculous to be moved to tears by a radio play or piece of music when you have suffered real raw tragedy.

Going back to places

Inevitably it is difficult to go back to places you used to go with your child. At first, I found it incredibly difficult to go into Isabelle's school and to go to events she had taken part in before and would have been part of now, had she been there. I found it very hard to go back to the hospital where she was treated. At the time of writing, we have not yet felt strong enough to visit the holiday home we had been to every year for the decade before Isabelle died.

When I feel nervous, I remind myself of the extraordinary bravery with which Isabelle faced her diagnosis and indeed, the bravery and strength and dignity she showed when the doctors told her there was nothing else they could do. I feel that if she could face all of that – the procedures, the pain and the loss – then I should be able to face difficult situations.

It is important to be able to go back to places and, indeed, sometimes necessary to do so. I believe, in time, you can conjure up the happy memories some places and events might invoke.

I have heard the phrase "high-functioning" in relation to an alcoholic. I think sometimes the best I can hope for is to be a high-functioning bereaved person, coping with the things I have to do and the places I have to go.

Doing stuff your child would have loved

So eventually you will find yourself going places and having experiences that your child would have loved. By the time you are out and about like this you probably will be strong enough to think, perhaps ruefully, how much they would have loved the experience. Inevitably you will also be sad that they never had the opportunity to have the experience. This will be the case even if it's only a tiny thing like watching the next series of their favourite TV programme. I suspect there will always be some regret that your child is not there.

> "HER ABSENCE IS LIKE THE SKY,
> SPREAD OVER EVERYTHING."
>
> CS Lewis

7

MEMORIAL AND COMMEMORATION SERVICES

We are not particularly religious people but sometimes a place of worship or a memorial event can be of comfort. Our local church holds a service – the Commemoration of All Souls – every year. Candles are lit by the bereaved in memory of their loved ones. It is a simple and beautiful service and whether the prayers speak to us or not, we have found attending such events of commemoration has given us space for a quiet period of reflection.

UCH ran a non-religious service of remembrance about seven months after Isabelle died. Again, candles were lit but also names, memories and thoughts were written on paper leaves and attached to a tree covered in tiny lights. It was terribly sad but also very beautiful.

We were so very sad to see parents there whom we recognised because that meant their child had not survived, but also we found it incredibly comforting to be able to share experiences with them and to remember our children together.

Indeed, talking to parents who have lost a child can be really helpful. They tend to understand in a way others simply cannot. You find you don't need to explain yourself. If there is a local group you can attend it might help. It's a club you never wanted to join but it may be a club that can support you. Your local hospice may run drop-in sessions. We found that just that single afternoon with parents at UCH really helped us.

If formal acts of remembrance are not for you, you can always do something privately or with close family periodically to remember your child. You could visit a place of significance to you or light a candle or throw flowers into a river or plant a tree. You might find it helps to have a period of quiet reflection from time to time.

Formal religions of all denominations have traditions for life events, often dating back many millennia. Even if you do not find the religious elements helpful, you might find the traditions give some structure or focus to your grief. At our local service for the Commemoration of All Souls, the vicar included the following words of the Iona Community, which I thought rang particularly true.

> "EACH OCCASION WE GLIMPSE THEM:
> THAT TURN OF A HEAD, THAT SMILE,
> THE WAY SHE WALKED, HIS SENSE OF HUMOUR,
> EACH TIME A KNIFE TURNS IN OUR HEART.
> IN TIME, THROUGH THE WINDOWS OF OUR TEARS
> WE SEE THEM AND SMILE.
> IN TIME, WE LET GO OF SORROW.
> IN TIME, BEAUTY AND MUSIC,
> REMEMBERED PLACES BRING SOLACE NOT PAIN.
> IN YOUR TIME, GOD OF ALL TIME,
> MAY WHAT WE HAVE SOWN IN PAIN BE REAPED IN JOY."
>
> **Surrounded by a Cloud of Witnesses:**
> Worship in the Celtic Tradition from the Iona Community

8

DEALING WITH DEATH – THE MYTH OF CLOSURE

As I have written this book, I have often thought that, as a society, we don't do death well. And we can do it better. In this digital age it sometimes seems we overshare. However, one of the good things to come out of this tendency towards transparency is that we are starting to talk about more difficult subjects like mental health and death. At the end of the day, everyone dies. Making sure we view grief as natural, normal and acceptable will enable those of us experiencing it to survive it. The bereaved should be able to say how they feel and seek help without judgement.

However, modern society is keen to solve problems. Bereavement is viewed as something you get through, as if there is an end point to be reached. The word "closure" sums up everything that is wrong with our attitude to mental health issues and, in particular, to the loss of a child. We want things sorted, packaged up and neatly put away because we are uncomfortable with raw emotion.

As you cannot ever get over the death of a child, you fail from the outset to satisfy society's expectation that people cope and are brave and can heal. Even quite sensible therapists and writers tend to talk about how long grieving takes and giving yourself time. Time wouldn't heal depression and it won't cure the loss of a child.

I would suggest you avoid anyone who believes or suggests that you can "work through the loss". I have said, I believe you never get over loss. The intensity of your feelings about the loss will lessen (you couldn't survive if the extreme pain and emotion and devastation of the early days continued unabated). However, you cannot – and surely would not want to – erase the emotional memory of your child.

You need to find coping strategies to help you survive when your emotional memories are triggered, whether by a particular date or event, or by a piece of music or a song. To fight, ignore or bury those emotional memories would be impossible, and even if you achieved such repression, I am not sure that it would be good for you. Many people have talked about losing their way many years after a tragedy because they repressed their emotions at the time. So, you should allow yourself to grieve. Society needs to allow you to grieve and to respect that grief. Society needs to accept the altered you because *you* have to.

Keeping their memory alive

I mentioned earlier that as part of recognising the importance of your child, you might want to increase the number of or update the photographs of them in the house.

You never forget your child. Remembering them and celebrating your love for them is so important. Your love will never end and this keeps the memory of your child alive.

> "UNABLE ARE THE LOVED TO DIE.
> FOR LOVE IS IMMORTALITY."
> Emily Dickinson

As time goes on, you may find it helpful or necessary to have some lasting physical memorial. If your child was buried, there will be a headstone. Isabelle had asked us to scatter her ashes somewhere beautiful – which we did – so we do not have a headstone to visit. Some friends got together and bought us the most beautiful metal sculpture. It is stunning and I think of Isabelle every day when I look at it. You might consider a bench somewhere of relevance to your family or planting a tree or a rose. One couple bought us a tree and when a friend lost her father, I bought her a tree – it had so comforted us to have a living memorial. Maybe you want to frame their football shirt or a poem of significance. If you need a memorial, create one that works for you.

I noticed that some friends and family literally did not say Isabelle's name. I found it important to talk about her and still do. I also noticed that some people would hesitate and almost flinch when I said her name or talked about her. The physical loss of someone does not reduce the huge part they played in your life and the love you feel for them. I have decided not to be over-sensitive to others in this regard – she was in my life and every waking thought for 17 years and it is inevitable that when talking about my life, I will include references to her. I am never going to be apologetic for, or embarrassed by, talking about her.

I will never stop loving Isabelle. The crucial point here is that parents love their children unconditionally, forever, and bereaved parents continue to do so.

9

YOUR RELATIONSHIP

As there is no rule book, no correct way to grieve or timing, it will not surprise you to find yourself out of sync with your partner. You cannot sing from the same page as there is no page.

They might be having a good day whilst you are having a bad day. They may be affected by something that – at least, on that day at that time – does not upset you. You might need to be quiet at a time they need company or to be busy. Men and women may grieve differently. One of you might want to seek out therapy or counselling, the other may not. One of you may need to talk, the other might want to be quiet and contemplative. When a couple loses a child, the intensity of the shared grief can be both physically and emotionally exhausting. Not that the exhaustion leads necessarily to sleep. On any given night, one of you might sleep whilst the other tosses and turns all night. All relationships, from friendships to marriages, require investment. Grief consumes you and you simply might not have the energy to make any investment in your marriage.

You might be annoyed with your partner that they do not seem as upset as you. Or you may feel guilty that you seem to be doing a little better than your partner. Grief is not a competitive sport. It is a dark and deeply unattractive thought that one person's grief is somehow more important than another's (although there are levels of grief – see the ring theory section). I think it is important to accept that the situation is awful. It is awful for both of you all the time. If you can be tolerant of your partner and their feelings, do be. You are probably getting on their nerves too.

Just as Kübler-Ross is often misinterpreted as setting out a five-step grief plan, the statistics about marriages surviving the death of a child are often misquoted.

In *The Bereaved Parent*,[11] Harriet Schiff suggests as many as 90% of all bereaved couples experience relationship difficulties after the death of their child. I have seen this statistic quoted as fact but cannot trace a source for Schiff's assertion. In 2006, The Compassionate Friends in the USA commissioned a survey[12] that suggested that actually a very small number of parents divorced after the death of a child. Fear of a failing marriage may add to your anxiety but the commonly touted, doom-laden idea that grief is a death knell for a relationship seems unfounded.

It is really important to remember your child. They live on through your love and in your life through memories. Talking to your other children and to your partner about the deceased child is part of this. So, you may feel fearful of losing the one other person that really knew your child and went through the loss with you. This alone seems like a good reason to value your partner and hold on to what you've got, even if that relationship is on the back-burner for a while.

The circumstances of your child's death may be such that you blame yourselves or each other. Former American president Dwight Eisenhower and his wife Mamie lost their son Doud (nicknamed Icky) to scarlet fever, contracted from a local girl hired as a maid. The Eisenhowers blamed themselves for Icky's death – if they had checked the girl's background, they would have known she had scarlet fever before they hired her. Stephen Ambrose, in his biography of Eisenhower,[13] explained how the strain affected them:

> *These feelings had to be suppressed if the marriage was to survive the disaster, but suppression did not eliminate the unwanted thoughts, only made them harder to live with. Both the inner-directed guilt and the projected feelings of blame placed a strain on their marriage. So did the equally inevitable sense of loss, the grief that could not be comforted, the feeling that all the joy had gone out of life. "For a long time, it was as if a shining light had gone out in Ike's life," Mamie said later. "Throughout all the years that followed, the memory of those bleak days was a deep inner pain that never seemed to diminish much."*

I think if you are in this situation, you may need to get professional help. Guilt (see Chapter Six above) is corrosive. The Eisenhowers lived in a different era, of course, when it would have been common to suppress emotions rather than discuss them. They did in fact stay together. Eisenhower recognised the simple truth about the loss of a child:

> "THERE'S NO TRAGEDY IN LIFE LIKE THE DEATH OF A CHILD. THINGS NEVER GET BACK TO THE WAY THEY WERE."
>
> Dwight D Eisenhower

Alternatively, your child may have died in violent or traumatic circumstances. Again, you may need help to deal with what is, effectively, post-traumatic stress. I discussed this earlier.

Even after a long illness, you may have questions about why your child died. One couple we met at hospital did not understand why their child had deteriorated and died so quickly. They went back to the hospital after their son's death to speak to the consultant and try to fully understand the circumstances of the death. This is an excellent idea. Obviously the death of a child makes no sense, but it must be of some comfort – and a good starting point – to fully understand what happened if you are to have some sort of life after it has been so cruelly shattered.

Some couples become closer through their shared grief. Bereavement, like any crisis, can have this effect. I felt our family pulled together really well during Isabelle's illness and following her death, and that we are closer as a result. Part of this closeness comes from the fact that only we truly understand the enormity of our loss and the sadness that flows from it.

Frozen in time

One of the hardest things about losing a child, as opposed to any other bereavement, is that your child is forever frozen in time. You do not know what they would have gone on to do or the person they would have become. You never knew them as an adult. You never saw them fulfil their potential.

This struck me particularly at the strangest of times – at a wedding. As we waited at the church, I suddenly realised we would never – in relation to Isabelle – be parents of the bride. Mark would never walk Isabelle up the aisle. He would never stand up at the reception and make a speech about how wonderful she was and how very proud we were of her.

I don't even know what she would have looked like. Would she have had children, travelled the world, fallen in love?

When you lose a child, you lose all the good times there should have been. In a way, this is why I do not think you can ever get over the death of a child – you live in a future that should have been theirs. There are so many memories you never get to make.

It is hard to know what is worse – the pain of what has happened or the pain of all the things that will never happen.

10

YOUR OTHER CHILDREN – SIBLING SURVIVAL

If you have other children, they will be profoundly affected by the death of their brother or sister. They will grieve and their grief will be unique to them and different from yours.

It is important to recognise that the loss of a child can change your relationship with your other children and their relationship with you. They may try to protect you from further sadness by hiding their own pain. Counselling is one option. Talking is always important – talk to your other children about their feelings and your feelings and about the child who has died. Try to keep the lines of communication open. However, your other children may be reticent to share how they feel out of fear of burdening you further.

As for parents – for some, it can bring you closer to your remaining children; for others, it can make you more distant. You might become anxious and overprotective. If you feel you are struggling with your relationship with your other children, again counselling might be the way forward. There may be an expert at your child's school. Or the school may be able to access support for your surviving children.

Going forward, it is important to ensure that bereaved siblings are allowed to be themselves. You invest all your hopes and dreams for the future in your child. When they die, you lose all those hopes and dreams. The remaining children cannot take these on – that would be an unbearable burden.

I have already discussed the research on the effect of the loss of a child on relationships. There is equally gloomy research about the effect of the death of a child on their siblings.

Most studies show negative effects, such as feeling sad, lonely, frightened and angry; experiencing guilt, anxiety, depression and sleeping difficulties; and fear of intimacy with others. Whilst not the most apparently erudite of comments, I am tempted to say, "No shit, Sherlock". Of course, the death of a brother or sister will seriously negatively affect the surviving siblings.

However, some of the research does seem to throw up some interesting points. The first idea that I thought of interest is that girls seem to be affected differently than boys. In *A Sibling Death in the Family: Common and Consequential* by Jason Fletcher, Marsha Mailick, Jieun Song, and Barbara Wolfe,[14] the writers note:

> *... sisters are far more affected than brothers in terms of more-severe reductions in human capital, residential/family status, and socioeconomic outcomes after experiencing a sibling death during childhood. This finding is both consistent with past research revealing that sisters form stronger bonds with siblings and also suggests an unequal family burden along many margins, such as caring for the emotional needs of surviving parents.*

I am not sure what you can do about this except be aware.

The second interesting idea is that the cause of death seems to affect how well a sibling copes. Not unsurprisingly, sudden violent deaths can be more detrimental than deaths after a long illness. Again, I am not sure what you can do about this except be aware, but maybe also consider counselling or support more suited to dealing with sudden traumatic loss if that is what the sibling has experienced.

The position remains that the surviving child or children will be deeply and uniquely bereaved. I was struck by the words of Lynne Shattuck[15] who has written about the loss of her brother: "I felt like our family had been a four-legged table, and one leg had suddenly been torn off. The remaining three of us wobbled and teetered. We felt the missing leg like an amputee, each morning waking to the horrible fact that Will was gone."

Siblings often form a little team, connected by their shared experiences of family life. The bereaved sibling loses that team and the person with whom they shared experiences and memories with. They also lose the person they were going to share the future with – Christmases, birthdays, weddings and so on. An unending list of days when their brother or sister will be missed.

Research suggests that many bereaved siblings describe themselves as feeling different from their peers. Obviously, their life experience is different. They may feel they have had to grow up quickly and sometimes abruptly. They may feel isolated. They are just not going to be as interested as they might have been before about whether they get chosen for the football team or in the intricacies of friendship groups. Adults will, of course, be more interested in them than before – relatives and parents and school teachers and professionals will be looking out for them. They may feel distant from children their own age and burdened by the constant attention and concern of adults.

Most of us look back on our childhood with a rosy glow. We remember hot summers, first kisses, sweets, building snowmen and carving pumpkins, mad relatives and family stories. I am keenly aware my surviving daughter will not remember her childhood with such carefree abandon. She has been denied something many of us take for granted.

My surviving daughter is keen to be judged on her merits and not to obtain any advantage from the tragedy she has suffered. But she will always be a victim of her "back story". She will carry the scar of her loss for longer than we will.

Family dynamics
In some cases, the death of a sibling may suddenly make the surviving child into a single child, or the oldest or youngest child. This creates a profound shift in their position in the family. Adapting to this position and coping at the same time with grief and sadness may be almost too much to bear.

When a family member dies, it changes the way the whole family functions. Children may not only mourn the person who died, but also the change in the family environment and the loss of the way things were and the way the family unit operated before.

We did not choose to have just one child and we would not have chosen for our surviving daughter to be a single child. I do not think of her as an only child – she is not and was not for much of her childhood. We cannot replace the very special role Isabelle played in her life or the great friendship she gave her. I think all we can do is talk and listen and support and love.

11

GRIEF, LONG-TERM

Whatever you do, however you feel, there will be a sense of something not being quite right. Some people describe it as feeling as if something is missing. Others describe a dull ache, which at times can sharpen. For me the feeling is as if my heart is heavy. I feel a weight all the time on my breast bone which sometimes becomes so heavy it is hard to breathe. The number of times I am "winded" by grief may lessen, but the strange heaviness remains.

> "WHERE YOU USED TO BE,
> THERE IS A HOLE IN THE WORLD,
> WHICH I FIND MYSELF CONSTANTLY WALKING
> AROUND IN THE DAYTIME
> AND FALLING IN AT NIGHT.
> I MISS YOU LIKE HELL."
> **Edna St Vincent Millay**

Forever, the fabric of your life has been changed. I remember a friend describing an unsatisfactory

Christmas. She had felt out of sorts but she prepared the Christmas lunch as normal, presents were given and received, fun was had by all, even my friend. And she would look back and describe it as a good Christmas, but she had felt at odds with the world and simply out of sorts. That's what long-term grief is like. You can still go to the cinema, see friends, shop, eat, drink but there will always be the background feeling that all is not well with the world and never will be. And the ache of loss will simply be the soundtrack to your life going forward.

Mark describes the feeling as walking across a frozen lake. Sadness is the great dark body of icy water beneath the ice. The ice is not uniformly thick. He feels as if, at any time, he could fall through the ice and be engulfed by the sadness, by the cold black water. Even when the ice is thick and he can walk across it with confidence, deep sadness is there just below the surface.

That may sound negative but it's not. First, you would not want to forget your child. And the price of carrying the memory of them and your love for them with you is that you also carry the loss of them with you. Secondly, while the pain never goes away, there will one day be laughter and friends and life in all its splendid forms.

Life, however, is fundamentally altered. You cannot go back to the way things were before. You simply can't, because it never will be the way it was before. You can stay in the same house/job/relationship, but life is different. You can view this as an opportunity to do things differently, or you can view just surviving and carrying on as success. But you must acknowledge the fundamental change in your life.

You may experience a feeling that you are always slightly distant from other people. Grief, the experience you have had of losing a child, can make you feel slightly set apart from other people. I had read (although as discussed above, it turned out not to be true) that many marriages fail after the loss of a child. I thought that this would simply be dreadful. Not only would you have lost a child but you would then lose the one other person who knew them like you did, who nursed them when they were ill or dealt with the shock of their sudden death, who went through those first agonising hours, days, weeks and months. Other than your partner, no one else really knows the details of the situation you are in. Of course, there are single parents who suffer the loss of a child – I cannot comprehend their strength. Even with a partner, you will experience the loss in your own unique way. This can make you feel lonely because you have a sense that no one understands you or how your life is. There is simply too much, and it is too hard, to explain to anyone else and no one will truly know what you have been through and are going through.

> "ON THIS BALD HILL THE NEW YEAR HONES ITS EDGE.
> FACELESS AND PALE AS CHINA
> THE ROUND SKY GOES ON MINDING ITS BUSINESS.
> YOUR ABSENCE IS INCONSPICUOUS;
> NOBODY CAN TELL WHAT I LACK."
>
> Sylvia Plath
> Parliament Hill Fields

The difference between your life experience and that of other people will always be there. This is the hardest thing in many respects. You may grieve for the loss of the "old you". You may be irritated by the superficiality of other people's lives. You may envy them for not having to suffer as you have. The loss of a child does change you. You will forever feel slightly different and distant from those around you. However, to some degree we all have a secret life – a feeling of inadequacy, unusual thoughts, self-doubt. We function with them and despite of them. So, despite the fact you feel separate from others, you can fully engage with others and with life.

The actor Jason Watkins said after the death of his two-year-old daughter that he did not want to be defined as being the man who lost his daughter, but as the man who coped with the loss of his daughter. For those of us who have lost a child, this is not a bad ambition: coping with the loss.

What I have come to believe is that we must, as bereaved parents, accommodate our loss, and society must allow the bereaved to accommodate their grief. In the days and weeks after Isabelle's death, a number of people advised me to seek counselling on the basis that they didn't want me to be like X: "she's still not right".

I wonder what is being "right"? I immediately thought that I would do it better, I would be "right". Really quite quickly, I realised that I would never be "right". I might function. I might laugh. I might work. But I won't ever be "right". Acceptance is the first step.

> "GRIEF HAPPENS IN THREE STAGES:
> THE BEGINNING
> THE MIDDLE
> THE REST OF YOUR LIFE"
> Candace Lightner

Time is no healer

I have hinted at this – I simply do not believe time can heal the pain of losing a child. In fact, as time goes on, I dread moving into years untouched by Isabelle. First, we are moving into times that she is not here to enjoy and that have no reference to her. The first New Year after her death was incredibly difficult – we were moving into a brand new year that she did not play any part in and that I had to begin without her. Secondly, we are moving further and further from our little family of four and all we had then. Those times are like a fading photograph that I cannot bear to fade any further.

Before she died (in June), Isabelle ordered and paid for a present for her sister's 16th birthday (in November). So, on that first birthday without Isabelle, her sister had a gift from her. Isabelle had also chosen a Christmas present for her sister, which we ordered. However, every birthday and Christmas going forward will be one without a gift from Isabelle. Every important date will be one without her or her influence. So, the passing of time is its own agony as it takes us further and further from the place where we want to be.

I heard an interview by Sue Klebold, whose son Dylan and his friend Eric Harris murdered 13 people at Columbine High School before killing themselves in 1999.[16] She considered moving away but realised that wherever she went, inside, she would always be the woman whose son killed 13 people. I feel the same – there is no point moving away or trying to escape in some way. Inside, I will always be a mother who lost her beloved child. I will always miss her and grieve for her and the life she should have had. I will carry the grief around with me and the loss deep inside me. Wherever I go and wherever I live, whatever I do, I will always be bereaved.

The sadness of outliving a child is one that remains with you all the time your child should be there – for the rest of your life. It is sewn into the tapestry of your life. It is like a colourwash – a filter through which you will always see the world. It will colour your every interaction and every happy occasion going forward.

However, the life you lead need not be without hope. In an interview of the children's author Michael Rosen by Stephen Adams[17], Rosen comments on the loss of his 18-year-old son to meningitis in 1999. Eleven years on, Rosen comments that the loss is ever-present, but the "relationship" he has with his dead son has evolved to one of acceptance and memories of the good times: "Now I do something and think, 'Eddie would have liked that'. And whereas in the past that would have been painful, these days I don't suppose it is."

As Isabelle encouraged us to do, one day I will remember her with a smile.

12

FINDING THE FUTURE

I started this book with a definition of grief and with the recognition that everyone's experience of grief is unique. When I was searching for that definition, trying to understand what I was going through, I read that the Ifaluk, a South Pacific people, use the word "fago" to express a feeling of compassion combined with sadness and love to convey their sense of grief. It sounds like a gentle, soft grief, and I think that's where I have come to rest. Every day I am wrapped in a soft heavy sadness. There are, of course, days when I am extremely emotional, times when I am distraught, nights when I toss and turn wracked with despair. The rest of the time there is just this deep, all-encompassing, never-shifting sadness.

On the day that a CT scan showed a tumour in Isabelle's lung and spots on her liver, I had to call Mark and tell him the news. At the end of the call I said: "I will never feel truly happy again." We had not even received a full diagnosis and I had no idea what lay ahead. But I just knew that true, carefree, unabandoned happiness would not be mine again. And so it has proved to be. This does not mean I cannot enjoy life. All of us can carve an existence out of the materials we are given. Do your best to sculpt a future. It will be a lasting legacy to the child you have lost that you live on, strengthened by the force of the love you felt for them, which is in part why you will always, always grieve.

Living a positive life

I hope I have not sounded overly negative – I honestly believe that accepting you will mourn the loss of your child forever is a good thing. It frees you up from the impossible challenge of overcoming the loss, it allows you to grieve, it allows you to keep the memory of your child alive and, ultimately, to celebrate their life and the joy it brought you.

Accepting that the loss of a child changes you forever will allow the new you to live, laugh and love in the future.

The new you does not have to change your life. You might want to carry on much as before. Or you might want to do new things. You might want to fundraise or volunteer or become a campaigner. Maybe you will want to exercise more or see more of those friends who have become particularly important to you. You may be pleased just to work or function as before. You may feel less afraid to challenge yourself and meet those new challenges with steely determination.

Although you will grieve the death of your child forever, this does not mean you will not experience happiness. Indeed, you may have a keener understanding of how important it is to embrace life. I feel I owe it to Isabelle to live a good life. I feel that I have to hold on to her memory and honour it. I take nothing for granted. I am not ready – and may never be ready – to party until dawn, but I try to appreciate the sun on my face, the friends I have, the happiness Mark and Isabelle's sister give me. Small, gentle, guarded joys may be all life offers me going forward. I'll take that.

But how?
I am a terrible public speaker. I am self-conscious and my nerves simply prevent me from delivering a speech or talk, even a vote of thanks, well. However, I have had to do it on occasion. One trick a colleague taught me was to simply pretend I was confident. It works to a degree.

When you are bereaved, you pretend all the time at first. You pretend you are fine, you pretend you are coping, you pretend to be interested. Over time you will find it requires less and less effort and you aren't pretending anymore. You are okay. You are coping. This is not you overcoming grief (we've talked about this – get over the idea of getting over it). This is you living with it.

At the beginning, you need monumental energy to hold yourself together, to put one foot in front of the other, to face the world. At some stage, you will find you require less energy. You go through the motions. Again, you haven't stopped grieving but you have started to accept the grief as your companion.

If you are struggling, here is what worked for me (much of which I have already discussed):

* Accepting that I will always grieve the loss of my child. I will always love her. I will never forget her (not for a waking second).
* Talking and thinking about her. This is partly in recognition of the fact I will always love her, partly in recognition of the joy she brought me, partly because she will always be a huge part of my life.
* Finding space. In this regard, do what works for you – prayer, meditation, exercise, therapy, yoga, manual labour, whatever. I took up running with Isabelle's sister and now run two or three times a week. It helps me feel strong and the physical exhaustion helps me to stay calm and to sleep a bit better.
* Taking nothing for granted. This works in two ways. Firstly, nothing about the future is certain. I know the worst can happen. So I am determined not to go into things half- heartedly. Secondly, happiness may come in the smallest things. As a result, going forward, I take joy in the little things. I try to appreciate them.

- Also, I really don't sweat the small stuff. Compared to all I am going through, it just doesn't matter. This takes away feelings of frustration and enables me to keep negative emotions in check.
- Treating grief as a *constant in* my life but not as my *actual* life. The focus of life has to be something else – family, friends, work, volunteering, personal or professional projects – and grief is the hum in the background.

I think about the many, many kindnesses during Isabelle's illness and how people rallied round her then, and us subsequently, and I am grateful and humbled and comforted. In the order of service we set out the names of those we were indebted to during her illness and on her death. Thanks to these people and to her friends, Isabelle knew how deeply loved she was during her lifetime – a gift many people never receive. And thanks to these people, we have survived and got this far. Be grateful, if you can, for the care of others.

I cope because I have others to care for and because I know Isabelle would want that (and more). I know she would want me to be happy. I am not there yet, but I can remember her with a smile (as she wanted) nearly as often as I remember her through tears.

13

NO RULES

As I have said, everyone says there is no rule book for grieving, no timetable and no right or wrong way. How unhelpful. I think there should be guidance both for the person grieving and those around them. There are rules for every other area of life. Humans like rules. Etiquette, manners, knowing how to behave oils the wheels of our lives. Therefore, it seems a shame that there are no rules to help at the most bewildering of times. Would they be so complicated?

For the griever
- Get help if you need it
- Develop coping strategies: routine, exercise, planned responses
- Be kind to yourself
- Tell people what you need (no more cottage pie)
- Accept the loss will change you and accept the new you
- In time, celebrate the joy your child brought you
- In time, carve out a new life with what you have, even though it is less than before

For friends of those grieving
- Accept that you do not understand – even if you have suffered a similar loss, it's not the same
- Ask what they need (no more cottage pie)
- Be kind, be reliable, be there, be a good listener
- Accept that whilst your life carries on, theirs is changed forever
- Do not impose a time frame on grief – the bereaved will never get over the loss of a child, they will just carry their grief around forever and may have tough days *for some considerable time, if not forever,* after the death
- In time, help the bereaved celebrate the joy their child brought them

Just imagine, right here, right now, that a call comes through that one of your children has died in a car crash. Imagine never seeing them again. No chats, no hugs, no texts, no laughter. Future plans ripped apart. No grandchildren. No wedding. The dynamics of your family changed forever. It is beyond comprehension. Therefore, we need rules to preserve the balance between the person whose life is destroyed and the person whose life goes on. I would say to friends trying to support someone who is bereaved that doing *something* is better than doing *nothing*. A clumsy hug is better than crossing the road to avoid the situation. Turning up, investing, is better than failing to be there for your friend.

In many ways, coping with grief requires acceptance (you are going to be sad) and permission (allow yourself to be sad). Helping a friend who is bereaved requires respect (respect that your friend is going to be sad) and permission (allow them to be sad).

THANK YOU

The 'Better Together' team (Lisa, Lynne and Simone) have been unwavering in their support. They have been there every step of the way, thoughtful, sensitive and incredibly generous. Thank you also to Sian MacDonald and to Louise Farrow, Annabel du Boulay and to my brother Peter and his family.

The Rev John Russell guided and supported us with sensitivity and gentleness. It is only with hindsight that we have understood the extent to which we are indebted to him.

The local community of Little Gaddesden has been generous to a fault, fundraising extraordinary amounts of money at numerous and varied events and supporting us with gifts, cards and food.

Berkhamsted School supported Isabelle throughout her illness, enabling her to continue at school right up until Easter 2016 and to fully take part in school activities and events. It is invidious to name individuals, however, it would be wrong not to mention Mr Petty, who was instrumental in ensuring Isabelle could continue at school and have as full and normal a school life as possible. He was central, together with Rev Jane Markby and Mrs Tracey Evans, in helping us arrange Isabelle's funeral at the school, and he has been in contact many times since her death. He has dealt with the most difficult of discussions with sensitivity. Mr Roland Maxted, Isabelle's former House Master, also enabled Isabelle to continue at school and was a steadfast source of support to Isabelle and to us. He undertook a skydive to raise an astounding £8,100 for the Teenage Cancer Trust. At Berkhamsted Girls' School, Mrs Richardson, Mrs McColl, Mrs Leonard, Mr Neill and all of her subject teachers supported Isabelle's sister and we are most grateful to them. Mr. Burchnall has gone over and beyond in his support of Isabelle's sister throughout Sixth Form and we are indebted to him.

The Hospice of St Francis Berkhamsted has provided Isabelle's sister and me with counselling. We are indebted to them for getting us this far.

During her illness, Isabelle had the best of care from the NHS Staff at UCH, from the consultants to the cleaners. The nurses, support staff and counsellors were professional and worked incredibly hard. She had access to some of the top people in their field, to groundbreaking science and to state-of-the-art equipment. Particular thanks to Dr Shankar and his team at UCH, Andrew Barlow at Watford General Hospital, Dr Jenny Gains and the radiotherapy team at UCH, and for the support Isabelle received from Laura Grey and from the lovely Charlotte Truss at Clic Sargent. The TCT unit at UCH is an unbelievably supportive facility. The Community Nurse Team at Hemel Hospital (particularly the force of nature that is Mary Heffernan) and the local Rennie Grove team enabled us to bring Isabelle home at the end of her life. We are indebted to all of them for the work they did for her.

We are also grateful to Dr Nigel Parker and Trizell for enabling Mark to spend as much time as possible with Isabelle.

SOURCES OF HELP

In crisis
Samaritans 24 hours a day, 365 days a year. (Tel: 116 123)

For bereavement support
Cruse Bereavement Care has a helpline open Monday–Friday (Tel: 0808 808 1677) and can provide national email support (helpline@cruse.org.uk) and face-to-face counselling with trained bereavement volunteers. They can also direct you to services local to you.

The Compassionate Friends (TCF) is a charitable organisation of bereaved parents, siblings and grandparents dedicated to the support and care of other similarly bereaved family members who have suffered the death of a child or children of any age and from any cause. (Tel: 0345 123 2304 or email helpline@tcf.org.uk)

Child Bereavement UK supports families and educates professionals when a baby or child of any age dies or is dying, or when a child is facing bereavement. (Tel: 0800 02 888 40 or email support@childbereavementuk.org)

The Lullaby Trust (previously known as The Foundation for the Study of Sudden Infant Cot Death) has a helpline and bereavement support services for families who experience the sudden loss of a baby or toddler. (Tel: 0808 802 6868 or email support@lullabytrust.org.uk)

Mind, the mental health charity, has a website listing many sources of help and a helpline open Monday–Friday. (Tel: 0300 123 3393)

Local hospices and charities specific to the cause of your child's death can help (such as Marie Curie or Rennie Grove).

Your GP or local hospital may be able to direct you to local bereavement services.

ENDNOTES

1 The Unnameable by Samuel Beckett (Faber & Faber, 1954).

2 On Death and Dying by Elizabeth Kübler-Ross (Routledge, 1969).

3 vmsave.petekeen.net

4 www.gov.uk

5 We Need to Talk is a coalition of mental health charities, professional organisations, Royal Colleges and service providers who campaign for better access to psychological therapies for people with mental health problems. Their 2014 survey of 2,000 people who had tried to access talking therapies within the last two years found: one third of people had to ask for therapy, rather than being offered it; half had waited more than three months for an assessment, with 1 in 10 waiting more than a year for assessment; only 15% per cent were offered the full choice of NICE-approved therapies; 56% were offered no choice of therapy; 45% didn't get the different types of therapy explained to them; half said they didn't get enough sessions to help them to recover; if the therapy

offered didn't work, 37% were not offered anything else; and, while waiting for therapy, 67% of people became more mentally unwell, 40% harmed themselves and 1 in 6 attempted to take their own life.

6 www.justgiving.com/fundraising/Izzy-D-Cancer-Is-Not-Me

7 The Sound of Silence by Simon and Garfunkel (1964).

8 BBC Radio 4, Friday 23rd September 2016. http://www.bbc.co.uk/programmes/p048lv9k

9 Finding Dory (2016), produced by Pixar Animation Studios and released by Walt Disney Pictures.

10 Traumatic Bereavement and PTSD. Retrieved 1st May 2017 from http://traumadissociation.com/traumatic-bereavement-ptsd-and-loss-of-loved-ones

11 The Bereaved Parent by Harriet Sarnoff Schiff (Souvenir Press Ltd, 1977).

12 A Survey of Bereaved Parents Conducted by Directions Research, Inc. for The Compassionate Friends, Inc. (October 2006): "Despite a widespread belief that the death of a child and the divorce of the parents are virtual cause and effect, this survey strongly suggests this to be a myth, confirming the results of the 1999 survey of The Compassionate Friends, as well as another study released the same year by two University of Montana professors. Survey group members were queried about their marital

status at the time of the death of their child, and those who were married were then asked their marital status today. Of 400 participating in the study, 306 were married at the time of the death of their child (of those who had only one child who died) or of any of their children (if they had more than one child who died). Of the 306 who were married, 57 (18.6%) responded that they were no longer married to the same person. Of that 57, eight were widowed, yielding a divorce rate of 16%, far below the national divorce rate of approximately 50%. Of those who divorced, less than half, only 40.8%, felt the impact of their child's death contributed to the divorce. Interestingly, of 67 persons surveyed in the 18–34 age group, 66 were still married to the same person, a 1.5% divorce rate."

13 Eisenhower: Soldier and President by Stephen Edward Ambrose (Simon & Schuster, 1990).

14 A Sibling Death in the Family: Common and Consequential by Jason Fletcher, Marsha Mailick, Jieun Song, and Barbara Wolfe (published online, www.researchgate.net, 2012).

15 When a Sibling Dies: The Loss of a Lifetime (published online in the Elephant Journal, www.elephantjournal.com, 19th February 2014).

16 A Mother's Reckoning: Living in The Aftermath Of The Columbine Tragedy by Sue Klebold (WH Allen, 2017).

17 Daily Telegraph 2011